INDIAN CUISINE

AUTHENTIC FLAVORS FROM THE LAND OF SPICE

CONTENTS

FOREWORD

After writing my recipes for this book, I visited India and decided to ask people in different parts of the country to define "curry" for me. Most people I asked struggled! It is not that no one in India knows curry; rather, it seems that they know it too well to call it something as generic as that. It means different things to different people.

Essentially, any fish, meat, or vegetables cooked with spices in liquid is a curry. The spices and liquid form a sauce that becomes a part of the dish. It is the spices or spice combinations that make each curry different. The cooking method itself varies from simple to sublime—in some cases, it could be as simple as simmering in a spiced broth, while in others, it may be a complex combination of frying, pot-roasting, and braising.

What is amazing is that, with time, this cooking style has traveled across the globe and exists in varied shapes and forms in so many different parts of the world. This is thanks to a migrant population that carried its traditional way of food and life with it. In fact, the journey of curry and its adaptability to its new environment plays an integral part in its success story.

While looking at the set of recipes in the book some 14 years after its first edition, I am delighted to be reminded of so many seminal curries, important cornerstones and classics of this genre of cooking that already feature in this book. Yes, 14 years is a long time, and trends have changed. There is a renewed appetite for vegetarian, vegan, and healthy options and a lot more interest, awareness, and understanding of the health benefits of spice. This book has an array of healthy, nourishing curries, as well as a balance of rich, indulgent dishes.

Indian Cuisine is a compilation of curry recipes like no other. What you will find in the pages to follow are some of the best recipes from different parts of the world, contributed by some of the leading experts from those regions.

Vivek Singh
2020

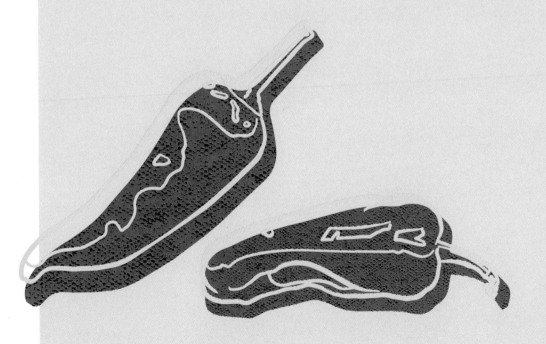

INTERNATIONAL INGREDIENTS

NORTH INDIA

The cooking of northern India has its roots in Persia, where the *tandoor* originated. The *tandoor* was brought to India by the Mughals, Muslim invaders who ruled most of India for almost 200 years, until the early 1700s. With the arrival of the *tandoor* began the great phenomenon of "tandoori" cooking, which has spread all over the world and, with the curry, come to broadly represent Indian cuisine.

Under some Mughal rulers, great levels of culinary sophistication were achieved. There were periods during which cooking flourished and its practitioners were nurtured like artists, enjoying a status similar to celebrity chefs today. Vast sums of money were spent on kitchens run by skilled master chefs, or *rakabdar*, as they were called. Each ruler aspired to outdo the other, in hospitality and in the dishes his chefs devised.

From this, it might seem as if all of North Indian cooking was influenced by Mughal rulers alone, but this could not be further from the truth. Like every cuisine, the cooking of a country or region is shaped by what grows there, the seasons, the climate, and the availability of ingredients, as well as religious and socioeconomic factors.

Rulers in some parts of northern India made great efforts to preserve their own culture and identity. They included the Rajput rulers from Rajasthan, who were avid hunters of deer, wild boar, partridges, and sand grouse, which is why this region has a fine tradition of game curries. In this arid desert climate, little grows, and cooking is earthy and rustic. Dried vegetables, roots, berries, and fruits are more common than fresh ones. Sangri beans, which need little water to grow, are much eaten. Rather than cattle and buffalo, goat and lamb are reared for both milk and meat. Yogurt is used for cooking and as a drink, as it has a cooling effect on the body.

Chickpeas, corn, and millet are the staples here, unlike the rest of the country. In such a dry climate this makes sense, because consumption of chickpea flour and cornmeal helps the body retain water.

Punjab, Delhi, and the rest of the north are relatively much better off in terms of fertile land, kinder climate, and better irrigation as a result of the five rivers that feed the region. This is a land of plenty, and plenty of milk, cream, butter, and other milk products are used; fresh vegetables, such as spinach, mustard greens, and fenugreek, are abundant; wheat is grown; and lamb and chicken are reared. Just about the best of everything is available and is used in the cooking in this region. The *tandoor* has had a major impact on the way of life here—even today, most households have a tandoori oven tucked away in their courtyard. If not, the village has a communal *tandoor*, where women will gather at midday or early evening to make their bread or simply exchange news and gossip. The mighty *tandoor* is so much more than just a means of cooking food—it is an essential part of the fabric of life in this region.

Bengal and the eastern states have very fertile land in the plains, as the Ganges River brings with it the rich soil from the north. The climate is mild, and monsoons mean that two crops can be harvested each year. One of them is rice. Local vegetables are plentiful; mustard grows in abundance, so mustard seeds and oil are used in cooking. With the proximity to the sea, fish is frequently used in Bengali curries.

When the British arrived in India, they made Kolkata—or Calcutta, as it was formerly known—their headquarters. As a result, British influences can be seen in some Bengali dishes (and vice versa). Kedgeree and Bengali

vegetable "chops" are just two examples of the crossover of cultures.

Today in northern India, 65 percent of the population is vegetarian, which explains why there is such a wide variety of vegetarian curries in the Indian culinary repertoire. The majority of North Indians are Hindus and Muslims, followed by Sikhs and those of other religions. Because cows are sacred to Hindus and pork is banned in the Muslim faith, beef and pork are rarely eaten.

While history, geography, and religion have all played an important role in shaping North Indian cuisine, there is one other important aspect—without which no cuisine can develop and survive—and that is creativity. And it is creativity that has enabled North Indian curries to travel all around the world, finding new homes wherever Indian migrants have settled. In adapting recipes to what is available locally, new curries have been created, but they are still identifiable as North Indian in their essence.

VIVEK SINGH

One of the things that makes North Indian cuisine so special is the spectacular variety of ingredients available to the cook. Each of the four regions has its own distinctly different cooking style, based on the climate and crops grown, religious influences, and the cooking mediums preferred. Everywhere the cooking is enhanced with fresh aromatics, herbs, spices, and other flavoring ingredients.

TASTE OF NORTH INDIA

RAW MATERIALS   **NORTH INDIA**

ASAFETIDA

This essential Indian flavoring, which is a dried resinous gum, has a very unpleasant smell and bitter taste, so it is never used alone, but when cooked in a dish, it enhances the other flavors. It is sold as powder, granules, or lumps and will keep well for up to a year. In addition to its culinary uses, it is supposed to be a cure for flatulence and to help respiratory problems like asthma.

BLACK LENTILS

Also known as black *gram* (or *ma* in the Punjab), these are primarily used whole in North India, most famously in a festive Punjabi dish with red kidney beans. Whole black lentils (*urad*) have a stronger aroma and richer, earthier taste than split black lentils (*urad dal*). Whole black lentils can be kept in an airtight container for up to 4 months.

CAROM SEEDS

Closely related to cumin, which it resembles in appearance and fragrance, carom seeds (*ajowan*) have a hot and bitter taste. However, when they are cooked with other ingredients, the flavor mellows. Carom seeds are particularly good in seafood dishes and with root vegetables.

CHAPATTI FLOUR

This finely ground whole-wheat flour is used to make unleavened breads (see recipe p.152).

CHICKPEA FLOUR

Also known as *besan* and *gram* flour, this is obtained from husking and then grinding split *gram* lentils (*chana dal*) into a powder. It is a very versatile flour, commonly used to make dumplings (p.36), in batters for fritters, and in bread doughs. Chickpea flour can be kept in an airtight jar for up to 6 months. Another form in which chickpea flour is available is *daria dal*, for which the split *gram* lentils are roasted before grinding. Roasting

Certain herbs and spices are integral to North Indian cuisine.
Dishes frequently include ginger and garlic, as well as both
fresh and dried chilies.

takes away the raw flavor and increases the flour's ability to absorb water. Roasted chickpea flour is often used as a thickener at the end of cooking.

CHILIES
Many different chilies, both fresh and dried, are used in North Indian cooking, varying in their fieriness and pungency. Kashmiri chilies, which are large and deep red, have a good flavor and color but are not too hot, and can be used in larger quantities than the smaller, much hotter green chilies. Whole dried chilies can be stored for up to a year in a cool, dark place (exposure to light will fade their vibrant color), whereas crushed or ground dried chilies will lose their power and spiciness after a few months.

CILANTRO/CORIANDER
In its leaf form, called cilantro, this herb is used to finish curries and as a garnish. The seeds, known as coriander, are used as a spice, whole or ground. Thought to have been cultivated for over 3,000 years, the plant is said to have a cooling effect on the body and an infusion is a cure for fever.

CINNAMON LEAVES
Although commonly referred to as "bay leaf" in Indian recipes, what is meant is actually the dried leaf of the cassia tree. I like to call it cinnamon leaf. Used in most dishes all over northern India, cinnamon leaves have a mild, sweet flavor. They are not edible, so they should be removed before serving. Should you find it difficult to obtain them, you can use bay leaves instead.

COCONUT
The hard, brown, hairy fruits of the coconut tree contain "water," which makes a refreshing drink enjoyed straight from the fruit. The crunchy, sweet white flesh is used to make rich coconut milk, which is an important part of many Indian curries. Freshly grated coconut flesh is used in Bengali cuisine, while desiccated coconut features in Muslim cooking.

FENNEL SEEDS
A very commonly used spice in India, whole or ground fennel seeds add a warm and sweet flavor to all kinds of curries. Fennel seeds are also used in pickles and chutneys and in desserts. Fennel is thought to have digestive properties, so roasted seeds are often served after a rich Indian meal.

FENUGREEK
The fresh leaves of this aromatic plant are eaten as a vegetable; when dried (*kasoori methi*), they are used to flavor all sorts of Indian savories and curries. (The best-quality *kasoori methi* comes from Qasoor in Pakistan.) The seeds of the plant are used as a spice. Ancient herbalists prescribed fenugreek to aid digestion, a remedy that continues to be used today.

GARAM MASALA
Garam masala, which literally means "hot spices," is a mixture of roasted spices that is used whole or ground to a fine powder. Each region of India has its standard version of garam masala, using the spices available and popular and the cooking of the area, and the recipes change according to individual taste. (See recipe p.167.)

GHEE
This is clarified butter, the pure butterfat, clear and golden in color. Traditionally in India, ghee is made from buffalo milk, which is higher in fat than cow's milk, and the process involves souring milk to make yogurt and then churning this to yield butter. Unsalted butter made from cow's milk can also be used for ghee.

GINGER AND GARLIC
After salt, these are probably the most-used ingredients in the cooking of Delhi and Punjab. They are added to marinades for meats, fish, and vegetables when preparing them for the *tandoor*, as well as being a flavoring in many curries. Ginger and garlic are normally made into a paste, which can be done separately or in combination: take about 4 oz (100 g) peeled fresh ginger and 3 oz (75 g) peeled garlic and blend with ¾ cup water using a food processor. The paste can be

kept in an airtight jar in the refrigerator for up to 5 days.

GOLD LEAF

This is the ultimate in exotic, luxury cooking. While edible silver leaf is quite commonly used to adorn dishes and decorate sweets in India, gold leaf is not as easy to find. Used as a decoration, it lifts up a dish in every sense.

KACHRI

A sour, tomatolike compound fruit native to Rajasthan, this has a hard skin and seeds inside. Available fresh and dried, it is used to tenderize meat and in the making of certain chutneys.

KASUNDI MUSTARD

This ready-made mustard paste is commonly used in Bengali cooking. It is made by soaking mustard seeds in vinegar, then grinding them to a paste with mustard oil and the addition of dried mango. Kasundi mustard adds its characteristic flavor to numerous dishes from the region. If not available, it can be replaced with Dijon or any other prepared grain mustard.

MUSTARD OIL

As the name suggests, this oil is extracted from mustard seeds. It is pungent in taste and smell and deep gold in color. Mustard oil is greatly favored in Bengal and eastern India, and certain Rajasthani dishes get their flavor from it. When used, the oil is normally heated almost to smoking point, then cooled down and reheated again, which tones down its aroma.

NIGELLA SEEDS

Although more commonly known as black onion seeds, this spice has nothing to do with onions and is actually the fruit of an herb related to the garden plant "love-in-a-mist." The small black seeds have an unusual, slightly bitter taste. Much used in Bengali cooking, nigella (*kalonji*) also garnishes many Indian breads.

PANEER CHEESE

An Indian version of set cottage or pot cheese, paneer is made by separating the whey from milk by adding lemon juice to curdle it. The solids are collected in muslin, tied, and pressed under a weight for a few hours to set—to soft curds or firm for slicing. On its own, paneer tastes quite bland. It is widely used as an alternative to meat in vegetarian dishes.

PICKLING SPICES

This combination of equal quantities of fennel, carom, onion, fenugreek, mustard, and cumin, either as whole seeds or ground, is used in pickles, as well as to flavor sauces and marinades for meat. You can buy ready-made pickling spices in India; elsewhere, you will need to mix the spices together yourself.

RICE

Rice is grown all along the plains of the Ganges, from the foothills of the Himalayas right down to Bengal in the east. Although basmati is the best known, there are hundreds of other varieties of rice available, patna being another notable one. In Indian homes, rice is most often cooked by the boiling method; pilau rice and rice cooked by the absorption method are reserved for special occasions, as they require more skill.

ROSE WATER AND SCREWPINE ESSENCE

Essences have been a part of Indian cooking since antiquity. During the time of the Mughal emperors, rare flowers were grown in the royal greenhouses to make attars, or fragrant essential oils, and some of these turned up in the kitchen. Floral essences such as rose water and screwpine essence (*kewra*) are the most popular today, used to flavor biryanis, pulaos, kebabs, desserts, and treats.

ROYAL CUMIN SEEDS

Also called black cumin, these spice seeds are very dark brown, long and very thin, and smaller than regular cumin. Their aroma is earthy and strong during cooking; the taste is nutty and warm. Royal cumin is used extensively in Kashmiri cuisine, and in Mughal cuisine as a tempering for meats.

SAFFRON

The costliest of all spices, saffron is the dried stigmas of a variety of crocus. Just a few saffron threads (stigmas) will give intense golden color and a unique, slightly bitter, perfumed taste to savory and sweet dishes. Store this precious spice in an airtight jar in a dark place to retain its color and fragrance.

SPLIT LENTILS

The most common variety of split lentils in India are *toor dal*, also called split yellow peas. They are used all over India to make the dishes known as *dals*. *Chana dal* are split *gram* lentils, a type of chickpea, from which the husk has been removed. A very versatile ingredient, *chana dal* are used in many ways in different parts of the country and are also ground into a flour (see opposite). *Masoor* or red lentils are the easiest to cook and digest and are commonly used to make lentil soups and *dals*, as well as kedgeree, which is essentially food for the infirm and children. When whole, *moong dal* (mung beans) have a green skin; it is these whole beans that are sprouted to use in salads and other cold dishes. Split, they are used in northern India for a variety of things, such as in the making of popadums, batters, and fritters, but *moong dal* are rarely cooked on their own.

TURMERIC

One of the most widely used spices in Indian cooking, turmeric flavors most Indian curries, be they meat, vegetable, or lentil, and also gives them a rich yellow-orange color. The roots (or rhizomes) are sold both fresh and dried, or ground to a fine powder. Turmeric has good preservative properties, too, so it is used in the making of many Indian pickles.

Grinding spices using a mortar and pestle

SOUTH INDIA

Southern India's ancient and deep-rooted cultural essence has been retained despite invasions, traders, religious conversions, and modernization. As with the rest of India, it originally consisted of many kingdoms whose Hindu and Muslim rulers fought wars to control the land and its resources. Many foreigners first touched Indian soil in the south, starting with the early Christians, and continuing over the centuries with the Portuguese, Dutch, Arabs, French, and, finally, the British toward the end of the 17th century.

After independence from Britain, southern India was divided on a linguistic basis into four different states: Andhra Pradesh, Tamil Nadu, Karnataka, and Kerala. The population was and is predominantly Hindu, just as in other parts of India, and as a result the cooking tradition is primarily vegetarian. Ayurveda (the ancient Indian medical system and way of life) has also had a great influence on the cooking culture. South Indians have great respect for the therapeutic value of food, and people follow Ayurvedic principles in their everyday eating. A traditional meal is more or less the same in most of the region: a large heap of rice on a banana leaf, with a variety of colorful vegetarian or meat dishes and pickles around it, arranged to balance flavors and provide nutritional richness.

New cultures and religions added new dimensions to South Indian cooking. Meat cookery was introduced by the Muslims in northern Kerala and Hyderabad and the Christian communities in Mangalore, Kochi, and central Kerala. Hyderabadi Muslim biryani is still the favorite biryani preparation for the majority of Indian people.

The cuisine in each of the four states has its own unique characteristics. Andhra food is considered to be the spiciest. Hot and spicy Andhra lamb and chicken curries are hugely popular with lovers of traditional Indian food.

The temple state of Tamil Nadu is renowned for its traditional vegetarian food and the most amazing variety of delicious snacks. The rice pancakes called *dosas*, steamed rice and lentil cakes called *idlis*, and popular train snacks like *vadais* and *bondas* are all contributions of the rich Brahmin (upper-class Hindu caste) community of Tamil Nadu. In the southern areas like Chettinad, meat and spicy-hot chicken curries are very popular, even though the majority of the people still keep to a strict vegetarian diet. The tangy flavor of *sambar*; spicy, peppery soups like *rasam*; and wonderful rice preparations with yogurt and sour tamarind are all examples of fine Tamil cooking.

Karnataka, home to the garden city of Bangalore, has a distinct culinary identity of its own. It is predominantly vegetarian, except for its border areas like Mangalore. There, the Christian and Anglo-Indian communities enjoy meat, just like people in the neighboring state of Kerala. Udupi, on the coast near Mangalore, is known for the cooking of its Hindu community, particularly famous for their *dosas* and other crispy pancakes. They also make tasty rice dishes like Bisi Bela Bhath (p.146) and Chitra Anna, which are finished with fresh colorful garnishes and savory tempering.

Kerala, on the southwest coast, is the most beautiful part of southern India. This lush, fascinating state is known as the spice capital of the country and has a strong tradition of Ayurvedic practice. It's no surprise that Keralan cooking is so healthy, colorful, and light compared to the rest of India. Kerala has a solid base of Christians and Muslims in addition to Hindus, plus a few surviving families from the Jewish community, and all these faiths add to the culinary diversity. In the north of Kerala, you find excellent Muslim meat cooking, whereas

Travancore, in central Kerala, has wonderful Christian chicken and lamb curries. Delicious seafood delicacies are prepared in the fishing communities along the coast, and the ancient Nair community is renowned for its vegetarian cooking.

In almost all the South Indian states, people prefer to use fresh ingredients like ginger, curry leaves, and coconut in their cooking, and these, as well as many spices, are grown in home gardens, as well as commercially to be exported to other parts of the world. Unlike northern India, where breads are often eaten with curries, people in this region like rice, preferring the local red rice to basmati for everyday meals.

In the villages, food is cooked in clay and earthenware pots, whereas affluent families use brass and silver utensils for everyday cooking. (These metals are deemed to be auspicious and to offer medicinal value.) Most of the dishes are stir-fried or boiled first and then cooked in coconut-based masala pastes. The final touch is to "temper" the dish with aromatic curry leaves, fragrant mustard seeds, and the sexy flavor of dried red chilies. The combination of these magical flavors is what makes South Indian curries so special.

DAS SREEDHARAN

Indian cooking is often thought to use a lot of spices and combinations of very intense flavors. But South Indian cuisine employs a much simpler collection of spices and flavorings. More than in the cooking of the north of the country, in southern India, great importance is given to the balancing of flavors. Subtle variations are created, and layering of spices makes the food lighter.

TASTE OF SOUTH INDIA

RAW MATERIALS   **SOUTH INDIA**

BLACK MUSTARD SEEDS
Black or brown mustard seeds are used in most savory dishes, providing a flavor that is typical of South Indian cooking. When the mustard seeds are fried in oil, often with curry leaves and dried red chilies, they release a very delicious aroma. Most recipes can be made without them, but they bring a special magic.

BLACK PEPPER
Known as "black gold," pepper is one of the most widely used spices all over the world. Kerala is considered to be its birthplace, because the plant from which the spice comes (*Piper nigrum*) is native to Tranvancore. Black peppercorns are the dried, almost ripe berries of the plant. Keralan pepper markets are attractive places to visit—the spicy aroma of the crowded markets is carried a long way. Black peppercorns can be used whole or ground for garnishing dishes.

CASHEW NUTS
Cashews are cultivated in South India and are often added to savory dishes, as well as being used in many snacks and almost all sweets.

CHILIES
In the traditional cooking of this region, there are several kinds of chilies used, including fresh green ones about 3 in (7 cm) long and dried red chilies, which can range in size from tiny and very hot to those that are larger and less hot. Chilies are famously known for their fiery power and people feel wary of using them, but you can control their heat by using them whole so they don't lose their seeds in the sauce. Or, if chopping chilies, split them and remove the seeds first.

COCONUT
Coconut is a very important ingredient all over the world, but most particularly in South Indian cooking. Freshly grated coconut is often ground with spices or dry-roasted for curries, as well as being

South Indian dishes use spicy, nutty curry leaves; earthy
fenugreek seeds; and creamy coconut milk, among other
fragrant ingredients.

used in savory snacks and many sweets. Unsweetened desiccated coconut can be used as a replacement, although it is drier in texture. Coconut milk and cream are also much used in South Indian curries, adding creaminess and sweetness.

CORIANDER SEEDS

Coriander seeds are part of most of the masala preparations in southern India, either dry-roasted or fried in oil. They have a very distinctive, strong flavor. Usually combined with fenugreek seeds, black peppercorns, and dried red chilies, they flavor many vegetarian and seafood dishes.

CUMIN SEEDS

This popular spice has a delicate character. Its mild pungency makes it a perfect component of many spice mixtures, including garam masala (p.167). Cumin seeds are also dry-roasted to sprinkle over rice dishes.

CURRY LEAVES

This is the most widely used herb in South Indian cuisine. As the name suggests, it smells and tastes like curry. While the flavor is spicy, it is also nutty, a quality brought out when the leaves are lightly fried in oil until crisp. Curry leaves can also be added to a dish just like any other fresh herb, whole or torn. Buy them whenever you find them fresh, as they can be stored in the freezer wrapped in foil or sealed in a plastic bag.

FENNEL SEEDS

In flavor, fennel seeds are similar to anise, and they look like slightly plumper, greener cumin seeds. They have a very strong flavor, so use them carefully and in small quantities or they will overpower lighter spices.

FENUGREEK SEEDS

This very bitter spice provides the earthy, musky curry aroma in many South Indian dishes, both meat and vegetarian. The seeds, which are angular in shape and yellowish in color, are added to pickles and chutneys, too. Use them in small quantities.

GINGER

This rhizome (underground stem) is used extensively in Indian cooking, and many people grow their own ginger so they will have it fresh whenever it is needed. Dried ground ginger is sometimes acceptable, but the fresh root is always preferred.

LIMES

Lime juice (and lemon juice) is used all over India to give an instant sour flavor to stir-fries and other dishes. The Indian lime is small and very aromatic, with a strong citrus flavor.

RICE

The traditional rice in South India is a red variety with a short, thick grain. It is not often found outside India. Fragrant basmati rice is considered to be the supreme variety and is reserved for special dishes. Mild-flavored rice flour is the main ingredient for making batters and doughs.

SPLIT BLACK LENTILS

Black lentils are very popular in many parts of India. In the north, they are used whole to make famously rich dishes, whereas in southern India, the lentils are usually skinned and split (urad dal). In many recipes, split black lentils are used as a spice, giving the dish a nutty flavor and crunchy texture. Their name is a bit confusing, because they are in fact creamy in color.

TAMARIND

This sweet and sour fruit is commonly used in South Indian cooking as a souring agent, and it brings a tangy contrast to mild coconut sauces. It's also used for chutneys and drinks. Tamarind pulp is sold in dried blocks and needs to be soaked in hot water to soften, then strained to yield tamarind water (p.172).

Whole and chopped red chilies

PAKISTAN

Pakistan is a country of over 208 million people and an area of almost 350,000 square miles (900,000 sq km). Through various invasions and occupations and through trade, it has been greatly influenced by its neighbors—India on the east, Iran and Afghanistan to the west, and China in the north, through the ancient Silk Road—and its culture, traditions, and cuisine have evolved accordingly over time.

The four provinces of the country, which range in terrain from very high mountains to the coastlines of the Arabian Sea and Indian Ocean, provide a great diversity of meat, game, poultry, fruits, and vegetables.

If given a choice, every Pakistani would eat meat every day. Lentils and beans are also sometimes used as the main part of a curry, but this is mainly for economic reasons, meat being more expensive. The favorite meats are lamb and mutton, although veal and beef are also eaten. Because Pakistan is a Muslim country, pork is never consumed. Various breeds of sheep and goats are reared in different parts of the country, most of them in a natural environment eating wild plants and herbs. Because they are pastured and organic, their meat has an excellent flavor. Chicken is the most popular poultry, while game birds such as quail, pigeons, and partridges are also occasionally enjoyed.

First-time visitors to Pakistan are always surprised to find so many fruits and vegetables. From the mountains to the plains, there is an abundance of cherries, apples, peaches, apricots, mangoes, oranges, and lychees, and from the coastal area come bananas and papayas. The array of vegetables includes potatoes, tomatoes, onions, carrots, peas, cauliflower, and many local varieties.

For everyday meals, Pakistanis add vegetables to meat—or meat to vegetables—whichever way you want to look at it. This is primarily to help the household budget, as it stretches the same amount of meat to feed more people. Meat is also added to beans and lentils, but to a lesser extent. One very popular dish is "chickpeas with chicken."

In Pakistan, the word "curry" is alien. *Salan* is probably the closest word for what is called a curry in India and the rest of the world. What makes a Pakistani curry different from an Indian curry is the regular use of meat and a limited use of spices. And unlike Thai curries, in Pakistan there is no added sourness or sweetness in the seasoning.

A very important rule to follow in making a good Pakistani curry is "less is more." Nothing ruins a curry faster than adding too many ingredients. Each ingredient is used for a particular purpose and is not duplicated with a similar ingredient. For example, if lemon is added, then vinegar is not required. Similarly, if fresh cilantro is used for flavoring, fresh mint is not needed. Each flavor can then be appreciated for its individual characteristics.

Another vital aspect of a good Pakistani curry is the freshness of the ingredients. Food is purchased each morning and eaten by the evening. At home, cooking is mostly done by women, and the recipes are passed verbally from mother to daughter. This makes Pakistani curries all the more interesting, because the same dish will taste quite different from house to house and region to region.

Traditionally, the curry cooking pot was made of earthenware, but today this has been replaced by a saucepan (without a handle). The first step in making a curry is almost always preparing the masala—cooking onions, ginger, garlic, and tomatoes with spices until the oil separates out. This is the basic foundation for most Pakistani curries.

Food colorings are not generally used in Pakistani curries, nor in tikkas and barbecued meats. Red color from red chilies and yellow from turmeric is all that is needed. Only rice dishes such as biryanis and some desserts are tinted with food colorings.

The predicament of a Western curry lover is often heartburn—when you eat a curry for dinner in a restaurant anywhere else in the world, it will still be with you for breakfast. However, this is not the case with a Pakistani curry. It is unique: fresh in flavor, based on seasonal ingredients for the very best taste, carefully spiced, nutritious, and economical to make. A Pakistani curry can be enjoyed every day and for every occasion.

MAHMOOD AKBAR

The key flavoring ingredients for a Pakistani curry can be divided into four groups. The first consists of the components of the masala base: onions, garlic, fresh ginger, and tomatoes. Second is spices, followed by fresh herbs and aromatics, and then salt, which is an essential seasoning for any curry. Careful balancing of these flavorings creates a foundation for the meat, legumes, and vegetables to be added.

TASTE OF PAKISTAN

RAW MATERIALS   PAKISTAN

BASMATI RICE
Probably the best rice in the world, basmati is the one to use for all Pakistani rice dishes, especially in biryanies.

CHILIES
The Dundicut is the most popular chili in Pakistan. Bright red to deep ruby red in color, it has a strong aroma and—Pakistanis think—a hot, pungent flavor (although in comparison with Thai and Scotch bonnet chilies, Dundicuts are quite mild). The heat level varies, ranging from 30,000 up to 150,000 Scoville units (the higher the number, the hotter the chili).

Dundicuts are commercially cultivated in Sindh Province. The total consumption of red chilies in Pakistan is about 400,000 lb (180,000 kg) per year, and over three-quarters of this is the Dundicut variety.

Red Dundicut chilies are rarely used fresh, but are usually dried and then ground into a powder. Red chili powder is considered indispensable for many dishes. As with other spices, chilies should be freshly ground, if possible. If you are buying red chili powder, choose small packets and do not keep for more than 2–3 months.

Hot and pungent green chilies are available fresh throughout the year.

Their size varies according to the season and where they are grown, but they are generally 3–5 in (7–12 cm) long.

FOUR SEEDS
This combination of dried, peeled seeds from various melons, pumpkin, and summer squash is used in chutney recipes (see p.178), as well as in halwas, sweetmeats, and desserts.

GARLIC
Because Pakistan has such hot weather, our garlic is more pungent than that grown in Europe. For all curries, garlic is pounded to a paste—usually with a mortar and pestle—to extract its full flavor and aroma.

As well as red Dundicut chilies, cooks use fresh green chilies in a variety of dishes alongside fresh herbs such as cilantro, mint, and fenugreek.

Garlic paste (and ginger paste, see below) can be made in larger quantities in a food processor and kept in an airtight jar in the refrigerator for 2 weeks. The pastes can also be frozen for up to 3 months; pack into an ice cube tray lined with plastic wrap and cover with more plastic wrap.

GINGER

Where onions and garlic are the basic ingredients in curries everywhere—and in much European cooking—almost no Pakistani curry can be made without adding ginger to this foundation, too. Ginger not only infuses curries with a warmth and earthy aroma, it also contributes positive medicinal properties. Only fresh, raw ginger is used, including for garnishing. It should be young, with a thin skin—older ginger has fibrous flesh. The skin is best scraped, not peeled. For many curries, ginger is pounded to a paste with a mortar and pestle; if very young ginger is used, the skin can be left on.

HERBS

In Pakistani cuisine, mostly fresh ingredients are used, and so it is with herbs, which have been used here for centuries. Cilantro, mint, and fenugreek leaves are among the most popular fresh herbs to add extra flavoring to curries and to garnish them.

ONIONS

The purplish-red variety of onion commonly cultivated in Pakistan is more pungent and lower in water content than European onions and is also less sweet, so onions do not impart a sweet flavor in Pakistani curries.

ROCK SALT

For seasoning curries, rock salt is preferred for its unique flavor, which is not overly salty or pungent. Rock salt is mined in abundance in Pakistan.

SPICES

The base (masala) of most Pakistani curries consists of fresh aromatics and tomatoes cooked with black pepper, red chili powder, turmeric, coriander, cumin, and salt. These spices are always added in small quantities, and each fulfills a unique requirement in the blend: black pepper provides the aroma and the bite, red chili the heat, turmeric the color, cumin the flavor, coriander the earthiness, and salt, of course, the savor. They don't duplicate each other, nor do they overwhelm each other. Other spices are added for particular dishes. For example, star anise adds an aromatic anise-licorice flavor to biryanis and other rice dishes.

While fennel, cumin, mustard, and fenugreek seeds are grown locally, most of the other spices associated with curries—like cloves, cardamom, cinnamon, nutmeg, mace, and so on—are imported from neighboring countries. In everyday home cooking, these spices are used only occasionally, and mainly whole rather than ground.

TOMATOES

The Portuguese introduced the tomato to the Indian subcontinent via Goa, and it took more than a hundred years for the tomato to spread from there and be accepted in the rest of the region. The Italian-type plum tomato is the variety most commonly grown in Pakistan, and it is in season from midspring until late fall. Although a staple in curries and every salad, tomatoes are not much used otherwise, except as a garnish. If tomatoes are not in season, you can substitute canned Italian plum tomatoes in the recipes.

YOGURT

Thick plain yogurt is added to curries to give a slightly sour flavor and to make them milder. Coconut milk and cream are never used in Pakistani curries.

RECIPES

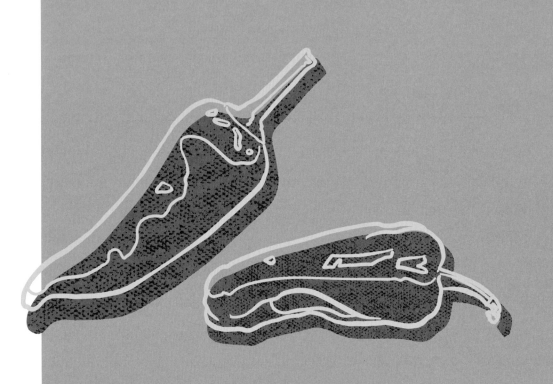

VEGETARIAN

This is a very unusual vegetarian dish using yogurt and chickpea flour as the primary ingredients. The texture of the dumplings and the complex mix of spices make a very interesting dish. This is good in the summer, served with steamed rice.

PITOD KA SAAG

CHICKPEA FLOUR DUMPLINGS IN YOGURT SAUCE　　　　　　NORTH INDIA—RAJASTHAN

serves 6
thin and sour

1 lb 10 oz (750 g) plain Greek-style yogurt
3½ oz (100 g) chickpea flour
1 tsp salt
½ tsp ground turmeric
½ tsp sugar
½ tsp ground garam masala
1-in (2.5-cm) piece fresh ginger root, finely chopped
2 tbsp ghee
1 tsp fennel seeds
pinch of asafetida
vegetable oil for frying

Yogurt sauce
2 tbsp corn oil
pinch of asafetida
½ tbsp cumin seeds
4 cloves
1 onion, finely chopped
7 oz (200 g) plain Greek-style yogurt
2 tbsp ground coriander
½ tsp ground turmeric
½ tsp red chili powder
salt and sugar, as needed
2 green chilies, stem removed and quartered
½-in (1-cm) piece fresh ginger root, julienned
2 tbsp chopped cilantro leaves
juice of ½ lemon

1 First, make the dumplings. Whisk the yogurt and 2 cups water with the chickpea flour, salt, turmeric, sugar, garam masala, and ginger in a bowl. Set aside.

2 Heat the ghee in a heavy pan, add the fennel seeds and sauté briefly, then add the asafetida and stir for 30 seconds. As the flavors are released, add the yogurt mix and cook, stirring constantly, for 20–25 minutes or until the mixture becomes thick and acquires the consistency of a soft dough. Remove from the heat and transfer to a greased 6-in (15-cm) square cake pan. Chill in the refrigerator for about 30 minutes or until set like a cake.

3 To make the sauce, heat the oil in a saucepan over medium heat and add the asafetida, cumin, and cloves. When they begin to crackle, add the onion and cook for 5–8 minutes or until soft.

4 Meanwhile, whisk the yogurt with the ground coriander, turmeric, red chili powder, and salt. Add to the onions, stirring constantly, and keep stirring as the mixture comes to a boil again, to prevent the yogurt from separating. Once boiling, add the green chilies and ¾ cup water. Bring back to a boil, then cook for about 5 minutes. Check the seasoning and add salt and sugar to balance the taste, if required. Finish with the fresh ginger, cilantro, and lemon juice. Keep hot.

5 Cut the dumpling "cake" into 1-in (2.5-cm) squares. Heat some oil in a frying pan and, when hot, add the dumplings a few at a time. Fry for a couple of minutes, until the dumplings have a crust. Serve on top of the hot sauce, or mix into the sauce and bring to a simmer before serving.

Panchmael means a mix of five, hence the name of this dish. It can be made with just three types of lentils—those most easily obtainable in large supermarkets and health food stores are red, *moong*, and *chana*. A visit to an Asian grocery store will enable you to find the others, but you can even make the dish with just one type.

PANCHMAEL DAAL

FIVE LENTILS MIX   **NORTH INDIA—RAJASTHAN**

serves 4
spicy, aromatic, and light

2 heaped tbsp split green lentils (*moong dal*)
2 heaped tbsp split yellow lentils (*toor dal*)
2 heaped tbsp split gram lentils (*chana dal*)
2 heaped tbsp split and husked black lentils (*urad dal*)
2 tbsp split red lentils (*masoor dal*)
1½ tsp salt
½ tsp ground turmeric

2 tbsp ghee
1 large onion, finely chopped
½ tsp red chili powder
1 tsp ground garam masala
1 tomato, chopped
1 tbsp chopped cilantro leaves
squeeze of lemon juice

Tadka
1 tbsp ghee
1 dried red chili
½ tsp cumin seeds
4 cloves
2 garlic cloves, finely chopped

1 Mix all the lentils together, then wash under running water. Leave to soak in enough cold water to cover for about 20 minutes.

2 Put the lentils in a saucepan with 2½ cups water, 1 tsp salt, and half of the turmeric. Bring to a boil, skimming off the white scum from the surface whenever necessary. Cover and simmer over low heat for 20–25 minutes or until the lentils, except the *chana dal*, are very soft and broken down.

3 Meanwhile, heat the ghee in a frying pan and, when hot, add the onion and cook until golden brown. Add the remaining salt and turmeric, the chili powder, and the garam masala and sauté for a minute, then add the tomato and cook until soft.

4 Pour the onion and tomato mixture over the lentils and bring to a boil. If the lentils begin to thicken too much, add some boiling water and keep stirring to ensure that they don't stick to the pan. Finish with the fresh cilantro and lemon juice. Remove from the heat and keep hot.

5 For the *tadka*, heat the ghee in a large ladle (or small pan) until smoking. Add the whole red chili, cumin seeds, cloves, and garlic in that order and in quick succession as the garlic begins to turn golden, then pour the contents of the ladle over the lentils and cover the pan with a lid. Leave covered for 2 minutes to let the smoke and flavors be absorbed by the lentils. Remove the lid, stir well, and serve immediately.

This is an earthy, rich Punjabi dish that is typical of the region, the land of five rivers. It is not for the calorie-conscious—it requires large amounts of butter and cream. You will need to go to an Asian grocery store to buy the specific type of lentil. The dish normally takes a lot of time to prepare—traditionally, it is put onto the embers of the coals in the *tandoor* and left to simmer gently all night.

DAAL MAKHANI

BLACK LENTILS   **NORTH INDIA—DELHI & PUNJAB**

serves 4
rich, earthy, and creamy

9 oz (250 g) whole black lentils (*urad*), soaked in lukewarm water overnight
1 tsp ginger paste
1 tsp garlic paste
1½ tsp salt

2 tsp red chili powder
2 tbsp tomato purée
⅔ cup salted butter
1 tsp ground garam masala
½ tsp ground dried fenugreek leaves
½ tsp sugar
¼ cup heavy cream

1 Drain the lentils and transfer them to a saucepan. Pour on 1½ quarts (1.5 liters) water and bring to a boil. Simmer for about 1 hour or until the lentils are thoroughly cooked but are not completely broken down and mashed.

2 Add the ginger and garlic pastes, salt, and red chili powder and simmer for a further 10 minutes. Reduce the heat to low and add the tomato purée and butter. Cook for 15 minutes or until the lentils are thick, stirring frequently. Take care that the mixture does not separate—that is, the butter does not separate from the lentils.

3 Stir in the garam masala, fenugreek leaves, and sugar, and adjust the seasoning. Stir in the cream and serve immediately.

A *kadhai*, or *karahi*, is the Indian wok, and this is the Indian answer to a stir-fry. The recipe here is probably the most popular of all *kadhai* dishes in India, by far the easiest, tastiest, and most colorful of the various different versions. This style of cooking is very versatile and quick if you've done some of the basic preparation—make a basic sauce in advance, and then it's simply a question of choosing your meat, fish, or vegetables and degree of spiciness. You may want to keep a jar of this basic *kadhai* sauce in your refrigerator. The *kadhai* method is becoming particularly popular with youngsters and people who are learning to cook and want to try out different things without spending a lot of time in the kitchen.

KADHAI PANEER

STIR-FRY OF PANEER CHEESE WITH PEPPERS   NORTH INDIA—DELHI & PUNJAB

serves 4-6
colorful, sweet, and sour

1 tbsp ghee or corn oil
½ tsp crushed dried chilies
2 red or yellow peppers, seeded and cut into strips, ½ x 1¼ in (1 x 3 cm)
1 red onion, sliced ½ in (1 cm) thick
1 lb 5 oz (600 g) paneer, cut into batons, ½ x 1¼ in (1 x 3 cm)
2 tbsp finely chopped cilantro leaves
½ tsp dried fenugreek leaves, crumbled
juice of 1 lemon
2-in (5-cm) piece fresh ginger root, peeled and cut into julienne

Basic kadhai sauce
⅓ cup ghee or corn oil
1 oz (30 g) garlic cloves, finely chopped
1 tbsp coriander seeds, coarsely pounded
8 red chilies, coarsely pounded in a mortar
2 onions, finely chopped
2-in (5-cm) piece fresh ginger root, finely chopped
3 green chilies, finely chopped
1 lb 10 oz (750 g) fresh ripe tomatoes, finely chopped
2 tsp salt
1 tsp ground garam masala
1½ tsp dried fenugreek leaves, crumbled
1 tsp sugar (optional)

1 To make the sauce, heat the ghee in a pan, add the garlic, and let it color. Stir, then add the coriander seeds and red chilies. When they release their aromas, add the onions and cook until they start turning a light golden color. Stir in the ginger, green chilies, and tomatoes. Reduce the heat to low and cook until all excess moisture has evaporated and the fat starts to separate out. Add the salt, garam masala, and fenugreek leaves and stir. Taste and add some sugar, if needed.

2 For the stir-fry, heat the ghee in a *kadhai*, wok, or large frying pan. Add the crushed chilies, pepper strips, and red onion. Stir and sauté over high heat for under a minute, then add the paneer and stir for another minute. Add the sauce and mix well. Once everything is heated through, check for seasoning, adding a touch of salt if required. Finish with the fresh cilantro, fenugreek leaves, and lemon juice. Garnish with the ginger and serve with *naan* (p.158).

Vegetables such as mushrooms and baby corn were not available in the past but are now more widely seen. Because this is a dish of mixed vegetables, feel free to use whatever you like. Just remember to cut all of the vegetables to more or less the same shape and size. Also, parboil hard vegetables beforehand and add the delicate and green vegetables later in the cooking.

SUBZ MILONI

SEASONAL VEGETABLES IN SPINACH AND GARLIC SAUCE   NORTH INDIA—LUCKNOW & AWADH

serves 4–6
fresh, light, and aromatic

6 oz (150 g) carrots, cut into ½-in (1-cm) cubes
6 oz (150 g) cauliflower, trimmed into ½-in (1-cm) florets
4 oz (100 g) fine green beans, cut into ½-in (1-cm) lengths
2¼ lb (1 kg) young spinach leaves
⅓ cup ghee or vegetable oil
2 tsp cumin seeds
1½ oz (40 g) garlic, finely chopped
1 large onion, finely chopped
1-in (2.5-cm) piece fresh ginger root, finely chopped

6 green chilies, finely chopped
1½ tsp ground coriander
2 tsp salt
4 oz (100 g) button or chestnut mushrooms, cut into ½-in (1-cm) cubes
2 oz (50 g) baby corn, cut into ½-in (1-cm) lengths, or canned sweetcorn (optional)
2 oz (50 g) broccoli florets, trimmed into ½-in (1-cm) pieces (optional)
2 oz (50 g) frozen peas, thawed
1 tbsp chickpea flour
2 tbsp butter
4 tbsp heavy cream
1 tsp dried fenugreek leaves, crumbled
1 tsp ground garam masala

1 Parboil the carrots, cauliflower, and green beans until al dente (3 minutes for the cauliflower and green beans, 4 minutes for the carrots). Drain well and refresh in ice water; drain again.

2 Blanch the spinach in boiling salted water until wilted, then drain and cool in ice water. Squeeze dry. Blend in a food processor to make a smooth paste, adding a little water as needed to liquefy.

3 In a heavy-bottomed pan, heat the ghee over medium heat. Stir in the cumin seeds, and when they start to crackle, add the garlic and sauté until golden. Add the onion, reduce the heat to low, and cook until soft and golden brown. Add the ginger and chilies and sauté for 2–3 minutes.

4 Stir in the carrots and cauliflower and cook for 2–4 minutes. Add the coriander and salt, then the mushrooms, and sauté, stirring, for 2–3 minutes or until they soften up. Add the baby corn and sauté for 1–2 minutes. Next, add the broccoli, beans, and peas. Mix together well. Add the chickpea flour and stir for 2–3 minutes, to cook off the flour. Add the spinach paste, then bring to a boil, stirring in the butter and cream.

5 As soon as the vegetables are boiling, check the seasoning and adjust if necessary. Finish with the fenugreek leaves and garam masala. Do not cook for too long after adding the spinach paste or it will discolor and make the dish unappetizing in appearance. Serve with paratha (p.154) or chapatti.

Most vegetarian meals in India often have a *kadhi* preparation, especially in the absence of *dal*. *Kadhi*, which is a yogurt-based gravy, is simple to make and has a balanced nutrition while being spicy. This is a Rajasthani preparation made with okra that is easily available in India.

BHINDI KADHI

OKRA IN YOGURT CURRY

serves 5
**slightly tangy and
  mildly spicy**

9 oz (250 g) plain yogurt
1 oz (30 g) chickpea flour
3 tbsp vegetable oil
½ tsp mustard seeds
3 sprigs of curry leaves, plus
  extra for garnishing
1 tsp ginger and garlic paste
3 whole red chilies

1 tsp ground turmeric
½ tsp roughly crushed
  red chilies
1 medium-sized onion,
  finely chopped
15 okra, washed, dried, and cut
  into 1-in (2.5-cm) thick pieces
½ tsp red chili powder
salt
1 tsp lemon juice
¼ tsp asafetida

1 Whisk the yogurt in a bowl until smooth. Add the chickpea flour along with ½ cup water and mix well to avoid lumps.

2 Heat 2 tbsp of the oil in a heavy-bottomed saucepan over medium heat. Add the mustard seeds and sauté. When they crackle, add the curry leaves, ginger and garlic paste, and whole red chilies and sauté for 20 more seconds, or until the ginger and garlic paste start to release flavor. Remove the red chilies from the saucepan and set aside for garnishing. Mix in half the turmeric along with the crushed red chilies and onion and sauté for 2–3 minutes or until the onion turns light golden brown. Sprinkle 2 tbsp water and stir constantly to prevent the masala from sticking to the base of the pan.

3 Fold in the yogurt mixture and cook for 6–7 minutes, stirring frequently. Reduce the heat to low and simmer for another 5 minutes. Set aside.

4 Meanwhile, take another saucepan and smear it with the remaining oil. Add the okra pieces along with the remaining turmeric, red chili powder, and salt and sauté for 2 minutes over medium heat. Sprinkle lemon juice; mix well; and cook, stirring frequently, until the okra pieces are tender.

5 Add the yogurt gravy to the okra and cook for 2 minutes, stirring occasionally. If the okra pieces are not tender enough, simmer for a couple more minutes.

6 Sprinkle asafetida and check the seasoning. Garnish with the curry leaves and the sautéed red chilies.

Morels, or *gucchis,* are rare mushrooms found in the Himalayan region. Loved by food connoisseurs for their flavor, these are mostly used in rice preparations and nonvegetarian dishes. However, they are also prepared as a vegetable, as in this recipe, and eaten with Indian breads or steamed rice.

DUM KI GUCCHI

STUFFED MORELS   **NORTH INDIA**

serves 5
mildly spiced and nutty

10 large dried morels
1 tbsp unsalted butter
salt
juice of 1 lemon
1 tbsp pomegranate seeds,
    for garnishing

Filling
½ oz (15 g) unsalted butter
2 tbsp broken cashew nuts
1 tbsp golden raisins
¼ tsp cumin seed
½ tsp finely chopped green
    chilies
½ tsp finely chopped ginger
½ tsp yellow chili powder
1 tsp chopped cilantro leaves
1 tsp chopped mint leaves
1 tbsp grated milk cheese
4 tbsp grated cheddar cheese
salt
¼ tbsp lemon juice

Sauce
3 green cardamom pods
3 cloves
3 cinnamon sticks
2 bay leaves
1 tsp ginger and garlic paste
1 tsp ground coriander
½ tsp Kashmiri red chili powder
½ tsp yellow chili powder
½ tsp ground garam masala
2 pinches each of nutmeg and
    mace powder
½ tsp crushed white
    peppercorns
1 tbsp brown onion paste (p.166)
5½ oz (150 g) plain yogurt,
    whisked
2 tbsp almond paste
3½ oz (100 g) tomato paste
¼ oz (10 g) grated milk cheese
2 tbsp light cream, plus extra
    for garnishing
few drops of rose water
pinch of saffron threads,
    soaked in water

1 Soak the morels in warm water for 30 minutes. Clean them thoroughly to get rid of any grit and trim off the stems.

2 Heat ½ tablespoon of the butter in a pan over medium heat. Add the morels and sauté. Sprinkle in the salt and lemon juice and cook, tossing occasionally (the morels will burn fast if tossed too much), until the morels are soft. Do not overcook, as the morels will lose their flavor. Using a slotted spoon, transfer the morels to a dish and set aside to cool.

3 To make the filling, in the same pan, melt the butter over low heat. Add the cashew nuts and golden raisins and sauté until the nuts are golden brown. Add the cumin seeds, green chilies, ginger, yellow chili powder, cilantro, and mint and toss for a minute. Add the milk cheese and sauté well, then add the cheddar cheese. Sprinkle salt and lemon juice and mix well. Transfer the filling to a plate and set aside to cool. Once cooled, stuff the morels with the filling.

4 To make the sauce, melt the remaining ½ tablespoon butter in the same pan over medium heat. Add the whole spices. When they release their flavor, add the ginger and garlic paste and sauté for a minute, stirring frequently. Sprinkle a little water to prevent the masala from sticking to the base of the pan.

5 Mix in the rest of the dry spices along with three tablespoons of water and cook, stirring occasionally. Add the brown onion paste along with ½ cup water. Cook for 30 seconds. Fold in the yogurt and cook for another 2–3 minutes. Add the almond paste—this will thicken the gravy.

6 Add the milk cheese and stir. As the gravy reaches a semithick consistency, fold in the cream and add salt if necessary. Sprinkle a few drops of rose water and the saffron threads, reserving the saffron-flavored water. Reduce the heat to low and slowly add the stuffed morels to the sauce. Cover the pan and simmer for 3 minutes.

7 Sprinkle the saffron-flavored water and garnish with a few drops of cream and pomegranate seeds. Serve hot with Indian bread or rice.

This recipe comes from the desert state of Rajasthan, famous for its dry vegetables, ghee, yogurt, and red-chili-based curries. Poppadum curry is a simple but flavorful dish that could be prepared any time of the year with ingredients that are readily available in most kitchens. Several varieties of poppadums, such as potato, *urad*, *jeera*, or plain, are available in the market. Prepare the dish with the one that suits your taste.

PAPAD KI SUBZI

POPPADUM CURRY   **NORTH INDIA**

serves 3-4
hot and sour

1 tbsp ghee
¼ tsp mustard seeds
3 whole red chilies
¼ tsp cumin seeds
2 sprigs of curry leaves
½ tbsp ginger and garlic paste
½ tsp ground turmeric
½ tsp red chili powder
½ tsp ground cumin
2 pinches of asafetida

9 oz (250 g) mildly sour yogurt
½ oz (15 g) chickpea flour
salt
6 split and husked black lentils
   (*urad dal*) poppadums

To garnish
½ tsp finely chopped
   cilantro leaves
½ tsp finely chopped mint
   leaves
½ tsp finely chopped green
   chilies

1 Heat the ghee in a heavy-bottomed saucepan over medium heat. Add the mustard seeds and whole red chilies and fry until the seeds crackle. Cover the pan with a lid if the crackling sputters out. Add the cumin seeds and toss until brown, then add the curry leaves and ginger and garlic paste and sauté for 2–3 minutes.

2 Mix in the turmeric, chili powder, and ground cumin and cook for another 2–3 minutes or until the spices begin to release their aroma. If necessary, add 2 tbsp water to prevent the masala from sticking to the pan. Sprinkle in the asafetida and cook for a minute. This will help enhance the flavor of the spices.

3 Meanwhile, whisk the yogurt in a bowl until it is well combined and thick. Add the chickpea flour and mix well. Add 1 cup water to dilute the yogurt mixture.

4 Slowly add the yogurt mixture to the saucepan, stirring constantly to prevent it from splitting. When all the yogurt has been incorporated, reduce the heat to low and simmer for 6–7 minutes, stirring occasionally. Add about ½ cup water and simmer until the gravy thickens slightly. Season to taste. The gravy should retain the sourness of the yogurt.

5 Roast the poppadums, one at a time, over medium heat or in an oven. Break the roasted poppadums into quarters and add to the gravy. Simmer for just 3 minutes. Do not overcook, or the poppadums will lose their crunchiness.

6 Transfer to a serving dish; sprinkle over the cilantro, mint, and green chilies; and serve with rice or any Indian bread.

Firdousi, a common item in most Indian restaurants specializing in Mughlai cuisine, literally means "heavenly" in Urdu. Any kind of meat cooked in this rich gravy tastes divine, and the erstwhile rulers often had it garnished with gold or silver leaves to signify its specialness. This dish uses *paneer* cheese, the vegetarian substitute for meat in most Indian preparations.

PANEER FIRDOUSI

PANEER CHEESE IN NUT GRAVY   NORTH INDIA

serves 5
rich, nutty, and creamy

3 tbsp vegetable oil
1 bay leaf
4 green cardamom pods
4 cloves
2 cinnamon sticks, each
    1 in (2.5 cm) long
½ tbsp ginger and garlic paste
3½ oz (100 g) tomato purée
½ tsp red chili powder
½ tsp ground cumin
½ tsp ground coriander
¼ tsp chopped green chilies
1¾ oz (50 g) brown onion
    paste (p.166)
1¾ oz (50 g) cashew nuts,
    ground with a little water
    to make a paste
½ cup light cream

salt
3 pinches of green cardamom
    powder
1 tbsp chopped cilantro leaves
generous pinch of saffron
    threads, soaked in warm milk
1 lb 2 oz (500 g) *paneer*, cut
    into bite-sized pieces

To garnish
10 cashew nuts, finely
    julienned
10 golden raisins, finely
    julienned
10 almonds, finely julienned
10 pistachio nuts, finely
    chopped and sautéed in
    butter until golden brown
1 tbsp chopped cilantro
    leaves (optional)
gold or silver leaf (optional)

1 Heat the oil in a heavy-bottomed pan over medium heat and add the whole spices. When they start to crackle, stir in the ginger and garlic paste and fry for a minute or until light golden brown. Add the tomato purée and stir for another 2 minutes.

2 Mix in the chili powder along with the ground cumin and coriander. Add 4 tbsp water and cook over medium heat, stirring occasionally, for 5 minutes or until the oil separates out. Sprinkle a little more water if you think the masala is sticking to the base of the pan. Add the green chilies and stir for 2–3 minutes or until the masala begins to release a spicy aroma.

3 Add ½ cup water and stir for 1 minute. Mix in the brown onion paste, cashew paste, and cream and cook for 3 minutes. The onion and cashew paste should blend with the gravy, giving it a thick consistency. Sprinkle in some salt to taste.

4 Add the cardamom powder, cilantro, and the saffron along with the soaking milk to the gravy. Slowly add the *paneer* to the gravy and cook for 1 minute.

5 Remove the whole spices and transfer to a serving dish. Garnish with the dry fruits and serve with *naan* (p.158) or *roti*. You could also garnish the dish with chopped cilantro and a gold or silver leaf.

A common preparation in Karnataka, mixed vegetables are beautifully cooked in a tomato masala that is flavored—unusually—with fennel seeds. It's much spicier than a lot of other South Indian vegetarian dishes, although coconut milk makes it creamy and slightly sweet. Serve this with paratha or chapatti, or as a side dish with meat and poultry curries.

RASA KAYI

MIXED VEGETABLE CURRY   SOUTH INDIA

serves 4
quite spicy and slightly sweet

3 tbsp vegetable oil
2 onions, cut into small pieces
1 green chili, slit lengthwise
4 oz (100 g) carrots, scrubbed and cut into 1-in (2.5-cm) pieces
½ tsp chili powder
½ tsp ground coriander
½ tsp ground turmeric
salt
4 oz (100 g) potatoes, peeled and cut into 1-in (2.5-cm) pieces
4 oz (100 g) cauliflower, separated into florets
4 oz (100 g) green beans (fresh or frozen), cut into 1-in (2.5-cm) pieces
½ cup coconut milk

Spice paste
2 garlic cloves, peeled
¾-in (2-cm) piece of fresh ginger root, finely chopped
1 green chili, finely chopped
½ tsp fennel seeds
4 oz (100 g) tomatoes, chopped

1 Grind all the ingredients for the spice paste in a mortar and pestle, or a blender or small food processor, until fine. Set aside and cut into 1-in (2.5-cm) pieces.

2 Heat the oil in a large pan, add the onions and green chili, and cook until the onions are soft. Add the carrots, chili powder, ground coriander, turmeric, and salt to taste. Mix well. Lower the heat and add the potatoes. Cover and cook for 10 minutes.

3 Add the cauliflower and green beans together with the spice paste and mix well. Cook, covered, for a further 10–15 minutes.

4 Remove the pan from the heat and slowly add the coconut milk, stirring to blend well. Serve hot.

All Keralan meals have two things in common: a yogurt curry and a *thoran* (dry stir-fried vegetable). A yogurt curry is a dish we look forward to, and it's one of the easiest to make, adding vegetables in season. Spinach is my favorite, while the red leaves in the beet family are very popular in our village. This is a mild dish, but can be made spicier if you prefer. Remember, though, not to heat it too much once you add the yogurt. A yogurt curry is always eaten with rice.

CHEERA MORU CURRY

SPINACH AND YOGURT CURRY   **SOUTH INDIA**

serves 4
lightly spiced and creamy

2 tbsp vegetable oil
½ tsp mustard seeds
pinch of fenugreek seeds
2 garlic cloves, finely chopped
3 dried red chilies
10 curry leaves
4 oz (100 g) shallots, chopped

3 fresh green chilies, slit lengthwise
1-in (2.5-cm) piece fresh ginger root, finely chopped
2 tomatoes, finely chopped
½ tsp ground turmeric
salt
4 oz (100 g) spinach, chopped
10 oz (300 g) plain yogurt

1 Heat the oil in a large saucepan and add the mustard seeds. As they begin to pop, add the fenugreek seeds, then add the garlic, dried chilies, and curry leaves and sauté for 1 minute. Add the shallots, green chilies, and ginger and cook, stirring occasionally, until the shallots turn brown.

2 Add the tomatoes, turmeric, and salt to taste. Mix thoroughly, then add the spinach and cook for 5 minutes, stirring occasionally.

3 Remove the pan from the heat and gradually add the yogurt, stirring slowly and constantly. Set the pan over low heat and warm gently for 3 minutes, stirring constantly. Serve warm.

A refreshing and light tomato dish, this is easy to make, and it's very versatile in that you can make it with other beans. I like to use my all-time favorite, black-eyed peas. Be sure not to overcook the tomatoes so that they retain their freshness. You can serve this with plain rice or chapatti to make a meal.

THAKKALI PAYARU CURRY

BLACK-EYED PEAS WITH SPINACH AND TOMATOES | **SOUTH INDIA**

serves 4
fresh, light, and creamy

3 tbsp vegetable oil
½ tsp mustard seeds
2 garlic cloves, finely chopped
10 curry leaves
⅔ cup chopped onion
2 green chilies, slit lengthwise
½ tsp chili powder
1 tsp ground coriander
½ tsp ground turmeric
7 oz (200 g) tomatoes, cut into
   small pieces
2 oz (50) spinach, chopped
4 oz (100 g) cooked or canned
   black-eyed peas
salt
10 oz (300 g) plain yogurt

1 Heat the oil in a large saucepan and add the mustard seeds. When they start to pop, add the garlic, curry leaves, and onion. Cook over medium heat for 5 minutes or until the onion is soft.

2 Add the green chilies, chili powder, coriander, and turmeric. Mix well, then add the tomato pieces. Stir well, then add the spinach. Cook over low heat for 5 minutes.

3 Now add the black-eyed peas with salt to taste. Cook for a further 1 minute or until everything is hot. Remove the pan from the heat and slowly add the yogurt, stirring well. Serve warm.

Okra and eggplant are the favorite vegetables for many South Indians, but in this versatile dish, you can replace them with your choice. I like the way the crunchy okra and juicy eggplant blend with the aromatic spices. This can be eaten as a main dish with paratha or as a fantastic side dish with meat and fish curries.

VENDAKKA VAZHUTHANANGA MASALA

OKRA AND EGGPLANT SPICY MASALA   **SOUTH INDIA**

serves 4
nicely spiced and dry

3 tbsp vegetable oil
pinch of fenugreek seeds
pinch of fennel seeds
2–3 cardamom pods
¾ in (2 cm) cinnamon stick
1 bay leaf
3 garlic cloves, chopped
2 onions, finely chopped

½ tsp ground turmeric
½ tsp chili powder
1 tsp ground coriander
1 tbsp tomato paste
2 tomatoes, finely chopped
6 oz (150 g) okra, cut into
  pieces
6 oz (150 g) eggplant,
  cut into pieces
salt
2 tbsp chopped cilantro leaves

1 Heat the oil in a saucepan and add the fenugreek seeds, fennel seeds, cardamom pods, cinnamon stick, bay leaf, garlic, and onions. Cook, stirring occasionally, until the onions are golden brown.

2 Add the turmeric, chili powder, ground coriander, and tomato paste and stir well, then cook for a further 1 minute. Stir in the chopped tomatoes and 2 cups of water. Bring to a boil, then reduce the heat and simmer for about 10 minutes or until the sauce is thick.

3 Add the okra and eggplant to the sauce with salt to taste and stir thoroughly. Cover and cook over low heat for 5 minutes or until the eggplant and okra become tender.

4 Garnish with chopped cilantro and serve hot.

This is a wonderful dish that's so easy to make, with a divine flavor. At home, we always relished simple stews with potatoes, but my mother liked to experiment by adding seasonal vegetables. This one was my favorite. You can replace the vegetables according to availability and to make the dish more colorful. Stew dishes are traditionally eaten with *dosas* and paratha.

KIZHANGU PAYARU STEW

POTATO AND GREEN BEAN STEW   SOUTH INDIA

serves 4
slightly sweet and very light

2 tbsp vegetable oil
1 tsp mustard seeds
2 dried red chilies
a few curry leaves
2 onions, chopped
½ tsp ground coriander
½ tsp ground garam masala
½ tsp ground turmeric

¼ tsp chili powder
2 tomatoes, quartered
10 oz (300 g) potatoes, peeled and cut into wedges or cubes
4 oz (100 g) green beans (fresh or frozen), cut into 1-in (2.5-cm) pieces
salt
¾ cup coconut milk
pinch of crushed black peppercorns

1 Heat the oil in a large saucepan and add the mustard seeds. When they begin to pop, add the dried chilies and curry leaves and sauté for 2 minutes. Stir in the onions and cook over medium heat for 5 minutes or until the onions are soft.

2 Stir in the coriander, garam masala, turmeric, and chili powder. Add the tomatoes and cook for 5 minutes. Add the potatoes and mix well, then cook over low heat for a further 5 minutes.

3 Add the green beans and salt to taste. Cook for another minute, then reduce the heat to very low. Pour in the coconut milk and ½ cup water. Stir well to combine. Cook for 15–20 minutes or until all the vegetables are tender. Garnish with the black pepper and serve hot.

Sambar is the most famous accompaniment for the traditional pancakelike breads called *dosas*, and it is the curry always served first at any feast in southern India. Sambar is made in hundreds of ways in the different regions, using a variety of vegetables and different roasted spices. It is a dish of the common man. Enjoy it with rice, *dosas*, or Akki Rotti (p.159).

KOOTU SAMBAR

VEGETABLES WITH LENTILS — **SOUTH INDIA**

serves 4
hot and tangy

4 oz (100 g) split yellow lentils (*toor dal*)
1 tsp ground turmeric
1 tsp chili powder
2 onions, cut into small pieces
4 oz (100 g) carrots, peeled and cut into 1-in (2.5-cm) pieces
4 oz (100 g) green beans (frozen or fresh), cut into 1-in (2.5-cm) pieces
3 tomatoes, quartered
4 oz (100 g) potatoes, peeled and cut into cubes
¼ cup tamarind water, made with 1 tbsp pulp and ¼ cup water (p.172)
salt

Spice paste
4 oz (100 g) freshly grated coconut or desiccated coconut
2 tsp coriander seeds
1 dried red chili

For tempering
1 tbsp vegetable oil
1 tsp mustard seeds
10 curry leaves
3 dried red chilies

1 For the spice paste, roast the coconut and spices until brown. Leave to cool, then grind in a food processor, gradually adding about 1 cup of water to make a fine paste.

2 Bring 1¼ cups of water to a boil in a saucepan and add the lentils, turmeric, chili powder, and onions. Simmer until the lentils are well cooked.

3 Add the carrots, beans, tomatoes, and potatoes and stir well. Cover and cook for 10 minutes or until the vegetables are tender. Add the tamarind water and salt to taste. Cover and cook for a further 5 minutes.

4 Stir in the spice paste. Bring to a boil, then reduce the heat to medium and cook, uncovered, for 5 minutes, stirring occasionally.

5 For tempering, heat the oil in a frying pan and add the mustard seeds. As they begin to pop, add the curry leaves and dried red chilies. Pour this over the curry and gently stir through. Serve hot.

This curry originated in Hyderabad, the seat of the Nizams, where food is judged not just by its *swaad* (taste), but also its aroma. Mirch ka Salan is a classic Hyderabadi preparation, with its characteristic tangy and mildly spiced salan or rich, velvety gravy. The sharpness depends on the type of chilies you use. It is advisable to use seeded green chilies to avoid a very hot dish. Interestingly, the use of sesame seeds, grated coconut, and peanut paste balances the sharpness of the chilies very well.

MIRCH KA SALAN

SWEET CHILIES IN VELVETY GRAVY   **SOUTH INDIA**

serves 5
mildly spicy and tangy

10–15 thick green chilies, each with ½-in (1-cm) stem
3 tbsp peanut oil
4 sprigs of curry leaves
½ tsp mustard seeds
¼ tsp cumin seeds
½ tsp nigella seeds
1 tbsp ginger and garlic paste
2 medium-sized onions, finely chopped
5 medium-sized tomatoes, puréed
½ tbsp red chili powder
½ tsp ground turmeric
1 oz (30 g) tamarind, soaked in ½ cup water to make tamarind water
salt
2 tbsp finely chopped cilantro

Nut paste
1¾ oz (50 g) skinless, roasted peanuts
1 oz (30 g) white sesame seeds
3½ oz (100 g) coconut, grated and roasted
½ oz (15 g) poppy seeds

1 Soak all the ingredients for the nut paste in 1 cup water for 1 hour. Transfer the soaked nuts along with the water to a blender and blend to a paste.

2 Clean and wash the green chilies. Slit open each chili lengthwise on one side and remove the seeds.

3 Heat the oil in a saucepan and slowly add the chilies. Sauté over medium heat until they change color and blisters form on the surface. Using a slotted spoon, remove the chilies from the saucepan and set aside.

4 In the same oil, add the curry leaves, mustard seeds, cumin seeds, and nigella seeds and sauté for 1 minute over medium heat. Once they begin to crackle, add the ginger and garlic paste and sauté for 30 seconds. Add the onions and sauté for 2–3 minutes or until golden brown. Mix in the tomato purée and stir for a few seconds. Cover the saucepan so that the flavors remain intact in the gravy and cook for 3 minutes or until the purée is well cooked, stirring occasionally. Now mix in the red chili powder and turmeric and stir for 1 minute. Pour ⅔ cup water and cook for 1–2 minutes, stirring constantly. Alter the quantity of water depending on how thick you like the gravy.

5 Stir in the nut paste and cook for 4–5 minutes. Add 5–6 tablespoons of water if the masala begins to thicken too much. Now mix in the tamarind water and stir for 5 minutes.

6 Sprinkle in salt to taste. Reduce the heat to low, add the sautéed green chilies, and slowly fold them into the gravy. Simmer for 10–12 minutes, stirring occasionally.

7 Transfer to a serving dish, garnish with cilantro, and serve with plain rice.

This recipe from the Iyengar community of Tamil Nadu is a must in any vegetarian spread during festivities and important dinners in South India. The dish is a tasty combination of green tender beans with spicy and slightly crispy lentils, cooked in a simple combination of spices.

BEANS USSILI

GREEN BEANS WITH LENTILS   SOUTH INDIA

serves 5
nutty and aromatic

½ cup coconut oil
1 tsp ground turmeric
salt
7 oz (200 g) green beans, cut in ¼-in (5-mm) cubes
1 tsp mustard seeds
3 sprigs of curry leaves, plus extra for garnishing
6 green chilies, slit lengthwise
1 tsp split black lentils (*urad dal*)

1¾ oz (50 g) freshly grated coconut
6 pinches of asafetida

Lentil paste
1¾ oz (50 g) split black lentils (*urad dal*)
1¾ oz (50 g) split yellow lentils (*toor dal*)
1¾ oz (50 g) split gram lentils (*chana dal*)
5 red chilies
5 pinches of asafetida

1 To make the lentil paste, mix all the lentils together and wash under running water. Leave to soak in cold water for 1 hour.

2 Strain the excess water and put the lentils in a blender. Add the red chilies and grind to a coarse paste. Add 5 pinches of asafetida, mix well, and set aside.

3 Heat the oil in a *kadhai* or wok over medium heat. Add the lentil paste and sauté, stirring frequently, for 7–8 minutes or until the lentils turn crispy and crumbly. Separate the excess oil and transfer the lentils to a bowl.

4 Heat 2 cups water in a separate pan and add half the turmeric, along with the salt and beans. Increase the heat and bring to a boil. Remove from the heat, strain the beans, and set aside.

5 Place the saucepan with the excess oil over medium heat. Add the mustard seeds and allow them to crackle for a few seconds. Add the curry leaves, green chilies, and split black lentils and cook for 2–3 minutes or until the lentils turn brown.

6 Mix in the grated coconut and sauté for 1 minute or until light brown. Stir in the rest of the turmeric and cook for another minute. Now add the boiled beans and the sautéed lentil paste and mix well. Reduce the heat to low, add the asafetida, and simmer for 3–4 minutes.

7 Pour ¾ cup water and simmer for another 3–4 minutes, stirring frequently, until it starts to sizzle. Garnish with curry leaves and serve hot with steamed rice or roti.

This curry comes from the southern state of Andhra Pradesh. *Pappu* refers to *dal* or lentils in this region, which is prepared with tomatoes and mild spices. While most recipes from this region are extremely spicy, this lentil preparation is an exception with its full and comforting flavor. You could alter the quantity of chilies to suit your taste.

TOMATO PAPPU

LENTILS WITH TOMATOES AND GARLIC   SOUTH INDIA

serves 4
slightly tangy and mildly spicy

5½ oz (150 g) split yellow lentils (*toor dal*)
2½ oz (75 g) shallots, each cut in half
½ tsp ground turmeric
2 medium-sized tomatoes, quartered
salt
2 tbsp vegetable oil

Tadka or tempering
3 tbsp ghee
½ tsp mustard seeds
½ tsp cumin seeds
2 sprigs of curry leaves
1 tbsp ginger and garlic paste
1¾ oz (50 g) shallots, chopped
5 garlic cloves, sliced
6 green chilies, roughly chopped
4 red chilies, roughly chopped
2 tomatoes, chopped
¼ tsp asafetida

1 Wash the lentils under running water. If you have one, put them in a pressure cooker along with the shallots, turmeric, tomatoes, salt, and oil. Add ¾ cup water. Put the lid on and pressure cook on high heat until it gives out 8–9 whistles. Remove the cooker from the heat and set aside.

2 Alternatively, leave the lentils to soak in cold water for about 20 minutes. Transfer them to a saucepan along with ¾ cup water, shallots, turmeric, tomatoes, salt, and oil. Bring to a boil, skimming off the white scum from the surface whenever necessary. Reduce the heat to low and simmer, covered, for 20–25 minutes or until the lentils are very soft and almost broken down.

3 For the *tadka*, or tempering, heat the ghee in a large ladle over medium heat. Add the mustard and cumin seeds and curry leaves and allow them to crackle. Mix in the ginger and garlic paste and sauté for 30 seconds. Add the shallots and stir-fry until golden brown, then add the garlic and sauté until brown. Throw in the green and red chilies and fry for another 30 seconds. Mix in the tomatoes and stir for 3 minutes. You could sprinkle a tablespoon or two of water to prevent the masala from sticking to the base of the ladle. Add the asafetida and stir. Now pour the boiled lentils in the tempering and mix well.

4 Add ½ cup water, cover, and simmer for 5–7 minutes. If the lentils have not already broken down, cook for another 15–20 minutes over medium heat. Check the seasoning and add salt, if necessary.

5 Serve hot with steamed rice or any Indian bread.

Although Pakistan is a meat-eating nation, various *subzi* (vegetable) curries feature very frequently in everyday meals. This curry is eaten on its own by the poor or as part of a meal by the more affluent. For a lot of people, it is the curry of choice, preferred over meat for its healthiness and taste, excellent served with fresh cilantro chutney (p.178) and roti. Almost any vegetable can be made into a curry, following the right technique and method. The key factors are to use very fresh vegetables and subtle spicing and to eat the curry as soon as it is cooked.

SUBZI CURRY

MIXED VEGETABLE CURRY   PAKISTAN

serves 3–4
fresh and fragrant

3 tbsp sunflower oil
1 large onion, finely chopped
1 tsp garlic paste
1 tbsp fresh ginger root cut in slivers
2 large plum tomatoes, peeled and chopped
½ tsp ground turmeric
1 tsp red chili powder
1 tsp cumin seeds
salt
1¼ lb (500 g) potatoes, peeled and diced
1¼ lb (500 g) cauliflower, cut into medium florets
5–6 tbsp chopped cilantro leaves

1 Heat the oil in a saucepan, add the onion, and cook until slightly browned. Add the garlic paste and ginger slivers, then add the tomatoes, spices, and salt to taste and stir well. Add the potatoes and cauliflower together with ½ cup water. Stir well, then put the lid on the pan. Cook for 15–20 minutes or until the vegetables are tender.

2 Remove the lid and continue cooking until the oil separates out. Stir in most of the chopped cilantro. Garnish with the rest of the cilantro and serve.

NOTE You can make this curry in advance and reheat it in the pan over low heat or in a microwave.

A typical family meal consists of a meat dish, a vegetable dish, and a dish of lentils or beans. This curry would be quite a common choice, because it is economical and ideal for winter or summer. It's also great for those who don't eat meat, because if served with garlic *naan* and a rice dish, plus cucumber raita (p.179), it makes a whole meal. The closest equivalent to what we call *lobia* are black-eyed peas, although you can also use other legumes such as red kidney beans (cooking time may vary, according to the bean you use).

LOBIA CURRY

BLACK-EYED PEA CURRY   **PAKISTAN**

serves 4–5
warmly spiced and earthy

3 tbsp sunflower oil
2 onions, chopped
1 tsp ginger paste
1 tsp garlic paste
3 medium tomatoes, peeled and chopped
1 tsp red chili powder
½ tsp ground turmeric
1 tsp cumin seeds
2 tsp ground coriander
½ tsp ground black pepper

salt
10 oz (300 g) dried black-eyed peas, soaked for 8–10 hours, then drained
¼ cup chopped cilantro leaves

To garnish
chopped green chilies
cilantro leaves

1 Heat the oil in a saucepan, add the onions, and fry until light golden brown. Add the ginger and garlic pastes and the tomatoes, and stir for a few minutes, then add the dry spices and salt to taste. Cook, stirring, until the oil separates out.

2 Add the black-eyed peas and stir to blend with the spice mixture. Pour in 3 cups fresh water and bring it to a boil. Put the lid on the saucepan, reduce the heat to low, and cook for 45–50 minutes or until the beans are tender.

3 Remove the lid and simmer over low heat until excess liquid has evaporated and the oil separates out. Stir in the chopped cilantro and remove from the heat. Garnish with chopped green chilies and cilantro, and serve.

NOTE You can make this curry in advance (it freezes well) and reheat it in the pan over low heat or in a microwave.

When you are not sure what to cook, or you have to prepare a meal in a hurry, potato curry is always the answer. It will never let you down. You can eat it for breakfast (serve it on toasted country bread, topped with a couple of fried eggs), lunch, or dinner, alone or as part of a meal, with any kind of bread or rice. It's great as a leftover, too. All varieties of potatoes can be used, even young new potatoes. This is true comfort food, delicious with apple chutney (p.178) and plain *naan* (p.158).

ALLOO CURRY

POTATO CURRY   **PAKISTAN**

serves 3–4
savory and comforting

2 tbsp sunflower oil
1 large onion, finely chopped
2 large plum tomatoes, peeled and chopped
8 red chilies

½ tsp red chili powder
1 tsp cumin seeds
salt
1¼ lb (500 g) potatoes, peeled and diced, or whole new potatoes
chopped cilantro leaves to garnish

1 Heat the oil in a saucepan, add the onion, and cook until slightly browned. Add the chopped tomatoes, then stir in the chilies, chili powder, cumin seeds, and salt to taste. Add ½ cup water and cook, stirring, until excess liquid has evaporated.

2 Add the potatoes together with another ½ cup water. Stir well to coat the potatoes with the spice mixture, then put the lid on the pan. Cook for 15–20 minutes or until the potatoes are tender but not breaking up.

3 Remove the lid and continue cooking until the oil separates out. Garnish with chopped cilantro and serve hot.

NOTE You can make this curry in advance and reheat it in the pan over low heat or in a microwave.

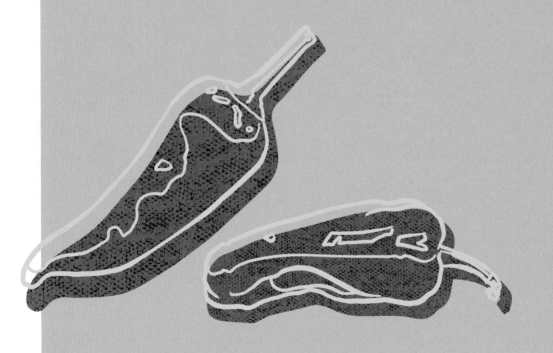

FISH

Northern India is not known for its fish dishes, but every region seems to have at least one standard recipe. Most of the fish used in northern India are river fish or are caught from lakes or ponds. Local fish include *rohu* or *katla* but elsewhere can be replaced by perch, barramundi, or prized varieties like halibut or monkfish.

DAHI WALI MACHLI

CATFISH IN YOGURT SAUCE   **NORTH INDIA—DELHI & PUNJAB**

serves 4
light, fresh, and slightly sour

2¼ lb (1 kg) fillet of catfish,
    perch, or carp, cut into
    1½-in (4-cm) cubes
1 tsp salt
juice of 1 lemon
1½ tsp ground turmeric
1½ tsp red chili powder
1 tbsp carom seeds (optional)
2 tbsp chickpea flour
vegetable oil for deep-frying

Sauce
3 tbsp ghee or corn oil
1 onion, finely chopped
1 tsp ground cumin
1 tsp ground turmeric
1 tsp red chili powder
1 tsp salt
1-in (2.5-cm) piece fresh ginger
    root, finely chopped
2 green chilies, slit lengthwise
16 oz (450 g) plain yogurt
⅓ cup chickpea flour
1 cup fish stock or water
½ tsp dried fenugreek leaves,
    crumbled
½ tsp ground garam masala

1 Set the oven to 275°F (140°C) before you begin to cook. Place the fish in a large bowl and rub with the salt, lemon juice, and turmeric. Set aside to marinate for 20 minutes.

2 Sprinkle the fish with the chili powder, carom seeds, and chickpea flour. Using your hands, mix and rub well to ensure that all the cubes of fish are coated with the mixture.

3 Heat oil in a deep saucepan. When hot, add the fish and deep-fry for 2–3 minutes or until golden brown. Drain on paper towels, transfer to an ovenproof dish, and place in the oven to keep warm while you make the sauce.

4 Heat the ghee in a saucepan, add the chopped onion, and sauté until golden brown. Add the cumin, turmeric, chili powder, and salt and sauté until the spices begin to release their flavor. Stir in the ginger and green chilies and cook for a further 2 minutes.

5 Whisk the yogurt and chickpea flour together in a bowl, making sure there are no lumps. Slowly add the yogurt mixture to the pan, stirring constantly to prevent the yogurt from separating. When all the yogurt has been incorporated, increase the heat and bring to a boil. Pour in the stock and bring back to a boil, then simmer for 3–5 minutes.

6 Add the pieces of fried fish and continue to cook over low heat for another few minutes. Check the seasoning, then stir in the fenugreek and garam masala. Cover with a lid to retain the aromas of fenugreek and spices and remove from heat. Serve immediately with steamed rice.

Bekti is a freshwater fish commonly eaten in India. There are two varieties. The Kolkata fish is smaller and has beautiful white flesh with a delicate flavor. It is considered far superior to its Mumbai counterpart, which is much larger, fattier, and considerably cheaper. Lake Victoria perch is a very good alternative to Kolkata *bekti*, but any meaty white fish such as halibut or cod could work just as well. If you wish, you can substitute ⅓ cup English whole-grain mustard for the mustard paste.

BEKTI JHAL DEYA

PERCH IN BENGALI MUSTARD AND ONION SAUCE · NORTH INDIA—BENGAL

serves 6
sharp, hot, and crunchy

2¼ lb (1 kg) white fish fillet, cut into 1½-in (4-cm) cubes
1 tsp salt
1 tsp red chili powder
1 tsp ground turmeric
vegetable or corn oil for deep-frying
3 tbsp finely chopped cilantro leaves

Mustard paste
2½ oz (75 g) yellow mustard seeds
⅓ cup white vinegar
1 tsp salt
1 tsp caster sugar
1 tsp ground turmeric

Curry
⅓ cup mustard oil
1 tsp black mustard seeds
3 red onions, finely sliced
2 tsp ground cumin
1 tbsp red chili powder
1½ tsp salt
1⅔ cups fish stock or water
3 tomatoes, cut into quarters and seeded
6 green chilies, slit lengthwise
pinch of caster sugar (optional)
¼ cup coconut cream

1 To make the mustard paste, soak the mustard seeds in the vinegar overnight. Drain, then grind to a fine paste. Mix together the salt, sugar, and turmeric and stir into the paste.

2 Rinse the fish under cold running water, then dry with paper towels. Season with the salt, chili powder, and turmeric. Deep-fry the fish in hot oil for 1–2 minutes or until golden brown, then drain on paper towels and set aside.

3 To make the curry, heat the mustard oil in a deep pan or flameproof Dutch oven over medium heat. When it starts to smoke, remove from heat and set aside to cool. Reheat the oil, then add the mustard seeds and allow them to crackle. Add the onions and sauté over medium heat for 5–8 minutes or until translucent.

4 Add the mustard paste and sauté for a further 5 minutes. Stir in the cumin, chili powder, and salt. Add the fish stock and bring to a boil. Reduce the heat to low and simmer for 2–3 minutes. Add the fried fish, tomatoes, and green chilies, and simmer for a further 6–8 minutes. Adjust the seasoning with salt (and sugar) if required and gently stir in the coconut cream. Garnish with the chopped cilantro and serve with steamed rice.

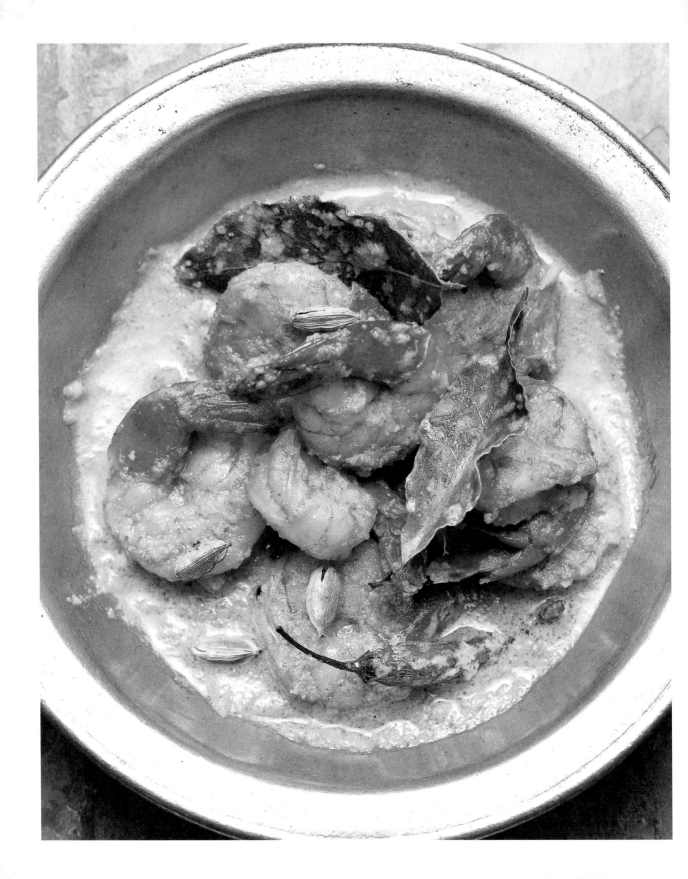

This is one of the all-time favorite Bengali dishes, reserved for very special guests, big celebratory buffets, and weddings. The curry is sometimes served in a green coconut, and the term *malai* refers to the creamy flesh inside a coconut. This is how most people think of the dish. There is a significant similarity between Chingri Malai Curry and a Malaysian *laksa*. The Bengali name may have its origins in the "Malaya," which is how Malaysia is known in India.

CHINGRI MALAI CURRY

JUMBO SHRIMP IN COCONUT CURRY SAUCE — **NORTH INDIA—BENGAL**

serves 4
rich, creamy, sweet, and spicy

2-in (5-cm) piece fresh ginger root, roughly chopped
10 garlic cloves, roughly chopped
6 onions, roughly chopped
1 cup vegetable oil
1¾ lb (800 g) jumbo shrimp, the largest you can find, peeled and deveined
1 tbsp ground turmeric

1 tbsp salt
3 cinnamon leaves or bay leaves
2 tbsp ground cumin
4 green chilies, slit lengthwise
¾ cup thick coconut milk
1 tsp sugar (optional)
5 green cardamom pods, seeds removed and finely ground in a mortar
2 tbsp ghee

1 Blend the ginger and garlic together in a food processor to make a fine paste. Remove and set aside. Blend the onions to a fine paste with ⅓ cup of the oil.

2 Season the shrimp with ½ tsp each of turmeric and salt. Heat 2 tbsp of the oil in a nonstick frying pan and sear the shrimp briefly, then remove and set aside.

3 Heat the remaining oil in a heavy frying pan and add the onion paste with the cinnamon leaves. Sauté over medium heat for 10 minutes or until light brown, stirring occasionally. Mix together the cumin, remaining turmeric, ginger-garlic paste, and ⅔ cup water, then add to the onions. Reduce the heat to low and cook for a further 5–8 minutes, stirring regularly. Stir in the remaining salt, the green chilies, and the shrimp and cook for 2–3 minutes.

4 Mix in the coconut milk and simmer for 2–3 minutes or until the shrimp are just cooked, adding a little more water if necessary. Adjust the seasoning with salt and sugar, sprinkle with the cardamom powder, and stir in the ghee. Serve immediately with steamed rice.

This would make a great party dish, one sure to impress your guests. In India, it is reserved for special occasions and intimate gatherings, when important guests and relations arrive. The use of coconut, mustard, chili, and ginger creates an interesting interplay of flavors. The sweetness of lobster and coconut is balanced by the heat from chili and ginger and the pungency of the mustard oil.

BHAPA LOBSTER

STEAMED LOBSTER WITH COCONUT, GINGER, AND CHILI   NORTH INDIA—BENGAL

serves 4–6
sweet, hot, and creamy

2½ oz (75 g) yellow mustard seeds

scant 2 tbsp white vinegar

6 raw lobsters, about 1 lb (450 g) each

1 cup thick coconut milk

3½ oz (100 g) plain Greek-style yogurt

6 green chilies, slit lengthwise

2-in (5-cm) piece fresh ginger root, cut into julienne strips

5 garlic cloves, blended to a paste with a ½-in (1-cm) piece fresh ginger root

2 tsp salt

1½ tsp caster sugar

⅓ cup mustard oil

1 tsp black mustard seeds

To finish

¼ cup finely chopped cilantro leaves

1 tsp ground garam masala

1 tbsp shredded fresh ginger root

1 Soak the yellow mustard seeds overnight in the white vinegar, then drain and blend to a paste.

2 Preheat the oven to 350°F (180°C). Slice each lobster lengthwise in half, leaving the head and shell on. Clean the lobster halves and dry on paper towels. Arrange the lobsters, shell side down, side by side in a casserole dish or roasting pan.

3 Whisk together the coconut milk, yogurt, chilies, ginger julienne, garlic and ginger paste, yellow mustard paste, salt, and sugar.

4 Heat the mustard oil in a pan to smoking point, then remove from heat and allow to cool. Reheat the oil and add the black mustard seeds. Once the seeds crackle, add the coconut-spice paste and bring to a boil over low heat, whisking constantly. Be careful not to let the mixture separate. Simmer gently for 2–3 minutes, then remove from heat.

5 Pour the sauce over the lobster and cover with foil. Cook in the oven for 15–18 minutes. Remove from the oven; sprinkle with the chopped cilantro, garam masala, and shredded ginger; and serve immediately with steamed rice.

In this recipe, shrimp are cooked in a sumptuous and velvety gravy with a touch of saffron and cream. The pomegranate marinade is the perfect tangy complement to the creaminess of the curry.

JHINGA DUM ANARI QUALIYA

SHRIMP IN POMEGRANATE AND CREAM CURRY   NORTH INDIA

serves 5
mildly spiced and creamy

2¼ lb (1 kg) large shrimp, peeled and deveined; set aside the shells, tails, and heads for the stock
3 tbsp clarified butter or ghee
1 tsp fenugreek seeds
1 tbsp ginger and garlic paste
1 tsp ground turmeric
1 large onion, ground
1 tbsp yellow chili powder
½ tsp ground garam masala
salt
1 cup plain yogurt, whisked until smooth
1 tsp ground fennel seeds
5 green chilies, each slit in half
4 tbsp fresh cream
pinch of saffron threads
3½ oz (100 g) fresh pomegranate seeds, to garnish
1 tbsp finely chopped cilantro leaves, to garnish

Stock
1 tsp black peppercorns
1 onion, roughly chopped
2 bay leaves
1½ in (3.8 cm) ginger, crushed
¾ oz (20 g) coriander roots

Marinade
1 lb 2 oz (500 g) fresh pomegranate juice
pinch of salt
2 tbsp lemon juice
1 tbsp red chili powder

Onion and cashew nut paste
2 medium-sized onions
scant 1 oz (25 g) cashew nuts

1 To prepare the stock, take a large saucepan and boil 1 quart (liter) water. Crush the shrimp heads, shells, and tails and add to the boiling water. Add the rest of the ingredients for the stock and boil for 20 minutes. Using a muslin cloth, strain the stock into a jug or pot and set aside.

2 Mix together the ingredients for the marinade. Add the shrimp and turn to coat them. Cover and set aside for 1 hour.

3 To make the onion and cashew nut paste, boil the onions with the cashew nuts in 1 cup water for 5 minutes. Leave to cool, then transfer the boiled onions and cashew nuts along with the water to a food processor and grind to make a fine paste.

4 Heat the butter or ghee in a large frying pan over medium heat. Add the fenugreek seeds and sauté for 30 seconds. Add the ginger and garlic paste, turmeric, and ground onion. Sauté for 2–3 minutes or until the onion is translucent.

5 Add the yellow chili powder, garam masala, and salt and cook over medium heat for 1–2 minutes, stirring continuously. Stir in the yogurt and cook for 1 minute. Add the onion and cashew nut paste, mix well, and cook for another 2 minutes.

6 Add the shrimp along with the marinade to the pan, cover, and cook over medium heat for 5–7 minutes or until the shrimp turn pink. Uncover and add the ground fennel seeds and green chilies, mix well, cover, and cook for 30 seconds.

7 Remove the cover and pour in the stock, mix well, and cook for 3 minutes. Add the cream and saffron and mix well.

8 Transfer to a serving dish and garnish with the pomegranate seeds and cilantro.

This popular recipe from Kerala boasts an exceptional balance of flavors, combining the tanginess of raw mangoes with the tenderness of fresh fish. It is often cooked in the Chavakkad region of Kerala.

MEEN MANGO CHARRU

FISH IN RAW MANGO CURRY   **SOUTH INDIA**

serves 5
spicy and sour

½ cup coconut oil
1 tsp mustard seeds
½ tsp fenugreek seeds
3 sprigs of curry leaves
1¾ oz (50 g) shallots, finely
   chopped
½ tsp ground turmeric
1 tsp red chili powder
1 tsp ground coriander
3 large-sized tomatoes, cut
   into quarters
2 raw mangoes, cut into
   2 x ¼-in (5-cm x 5-mm)
   thick pieces

⅔ cup tamarind pulp
salt
2¼ lb (1 kg) fillets of sole
   or catfish, cut into chunks
7 oz (200 g) coconut paste
1 tsp chopped cilantro leaves,
   to garnish

Spice mix
½ tsp black peppercorns
15 garlic cloves
1 tsp cumin seeds
4 whole red chilies

1 For the spice mix, roughly grind the peppercorns, garlic, cumin, and whole red chilies in a food processor and set aside.

2 Heat the oil in a heavy-bottomed pan over medium heat, add the mustard seeds, and reduce the heat once they start crackling. Add the fenugreek seeds and curry leaves and sauté for 20 seconds.

3 Add the shallots and sauté for 1 minute or until golden brown. Increase the heat to medium-high, add the spice mix, and sauté for 1–2 minutes. Add the turmeric, chili powder, and coriander and sauté for 30 seconds. Add the tomatoes and raw mangoes and cook for 2 minutes. Mix in the tamarind pulp and salt, cover, and cook for 3 minutes.

4 Uncover and carefully add the fish chunks along with ⅔ cup water. Cover with the lid and cook for 5 minutes.

5 Once the fish is almost done, mix in the coconut paste and simmer for 5 minutes. Turn over the fish chunks to mix well; be careful not to break them. Check the consistency of the gravy and add 4–5 tablespoons of water if necessary.

6 Transfer to a serving dish, garnish with the cilantro, and serve hot with plain rice or *idlis*.

In Sri Lanka, as along the South Indian coast, fish is more popular than meat or chicken, and many of the dishes and cooking techniques on this beautiful island are similar to those in southern India. A wide variety of fresh seafood can be found in the markets. This tasty curry is common to many communities in Sri Lanka. It goes well with tamarind rice (p.148) or a simple bread like Akki Rotti (p.159).

MEEN KARI

SRI LANKAN FISH STEW

SOUTH INDIA

serves 4
deliciously spiced

1 tbsp ghee or butter
12 shallots, cut into wedges
1½ tsp all-purpose flour
3 tbsp tomato paste
½ tsp chili powder
½ tsp ground coriander

¼ tsp ground turmeric
salt
14 oz (400 g) kingfish or salmon fillet, skinned and cut into small pieces
1 cup thick coconut milk
1 tbsp wine or cider vinegar
pinch of crushed black peppercorns

1 Heat the ghee or butter in a large saucepan, add the shallots, and fry for 5 minutes or until brown. Remove the pan from the heat and sprinkle the flour over the shallots. Mix well, then return to low heat.

2 Slowly add 2 cups water, mixing well to avoid lumps. Stir in the tomato paste, chili powder, coriander, turmeric, and some salt. Bring to a boil, stirring well, then add the fish. Simmer gently, covered, for 20 minutes or until the fish is cooked, stirring occasionally.

3 Remove the pan from the heat. Pour in the coconut milk and stir for 2 minutes. Add the vinegar and sprinkle with the crushed black pepper. Serve immediately.

Giant tamarind trees grow everywhere in southern India, offering shade from the sun and their fruits for cooking. The sweet and sour flavor of tamarind is found in all kinds of dishes, from the fruity sweets loved by schoolchildren to curries such as this one. Millions of people in the fishing communities eat fish cooked in terra-cotta pots with red chilies and tamarind. Serve this curry with plain rice.

MADRAS MEEN KOLAMBU

TAMARIND FISH CURRY   **SOUTH INDIA**

serves 6
sweet and sour

2 tbsp vegetable oil
1 tsp mustard seeds
10 curry leaves
pinch of fenugreek seeds
2 garlic cloves, chopped
2 onions, chopped

¼ tsp ground turmeric
½ tsp chili powder
3 tomatoes, chopped
1 tsp tomato paste
sea salt
½ cup tamarind water, made
  with 1¾ oz (50 g) pulp and
  ½ cup water (p.172)
1¼ lb (500 g) lemon sole fillets

1 Heat the oil in a large saucepan. Add the mustard seeds and, when they begin to pop, add the curry leaves, fenugreek seeds, and garlic. Sauté for 1–2 minutes or until the garlic turns brown. Stir in the onions and cook over medium heat, stirring occasionally, for 10 minutes or until they are golden.

2 Add the turmeric and chili powder and mix well, then add the chopped tomatoes, tomato paste, and some salt and cook for a further 2 minutes. Pour in the tamarind water and ¾ cup water. Bring the mixture to a boil and simmer for 12 minutes, stirring occasionally, until the sauce thickens.

3 Cut the fish fillets into pieces and carefully mix into the sauce. Lower the heat and cook gently for 4–5 minutes or until the fish is just cooked through. Serve immediately.

This is a traditional fish curry from the region of Travancore, in southern Kerala, one of the most beautiful parts of southern India, where the coastal lowlands on the Arabian Sea are surrounded by lagoons. This is a fantastic dish for people who like mild curries. The creamy, smooth flavor will balance spicier dishes. Serve with plain rice or any Indian bread.

ARACHU VECHA CURRY

COCONUT FISH CURRY

SOUTH INDIA

serves 6
**mild, creamy, nutty,
and aromatic**

2 tbsp vegetable oil
7 oz (200 g) shallots, chopped
10 curry leaves
1¼ lb (500 g) tilapia or other
   white fish fillets, skinned
1 tbsp lemon juice

Spice paste
4 oz (100 g) freshly grated
   coconut
1 tsp ground coriander
½ tsp chili powder
large pinch of ground turmeric

1 To make the spice paste, put the coconut, ground coriander, chili powder, and turmeric in a blender. Pour in ¾ cup water and process for 2–3 minutes to make a smooth paste. Set aside.

2 Heat the oil in a large frying pan, *karahi*, or wok. Add the shallots and curry leaves and cook over medium-low heat for 5 minutes or until the shallots are soft. Stir in the coconut spice paste together with ¾ cup water and bring the mixture to a boil. Cook for about 5 minutes, stirring occasionally, until the sauce has thickened.

3 Cut the fish fillets into 1-in (2.5-cm) pieces and add to the sauce. Pour in the lemon juice and mix carefully. Cook gently for 4–5 minutes or until the fish is cooked through. Remove the pan from the heat and serve immediately.

Eating a fish curry at least once a day is a must for the majority of South Indians who live on the coast. Kingfish is very popular and versatile. Its rich flavor works well with the tamarind and coconut milk combination here, which is typical of the region. Many of the fish dishes are simple and prepared for daily meals, whereas this curry would be made for a festival or other special occasion.

NADAN MEEN KOOTAN

KINGFISH CURRY

SOUTH INDIA

serves 4–6
sour and spicy

2 tbsp vegetable oil
½ tsp mustard seeds
10 curry leaves
pinch of fenugreek seeds
1 large onion, chopped
1-in (2.5-cm) piece fresh ginger root, thinly sliced
½ tsp ground turmeric
½ tsp chili powder

1 tsp ground coriander
2 tomatoes, chopped
sea salt
3 tbsp tamarind water, made with 1 tbsp pulp and 3 tbsp water (p.172)
1¼ lb (500 g) kingfish fillet, skinned and cut into 1½-in (4-cm) pieces
¾ cup thick coconut milk
pinch of crushed black peppercorns

1 Heat the oil in a large saucepan, *karahi*, or wok. Add the mustard seeds, and when they start to pop, add the curry leaves and fenugreek seeds. Sauté for 1 minute or until the fenugreek seeds turn golden, then add the onion and cook for 5 minutes over medium heat, stirring occasionally.

2 Add the ginger, turmeric, chili powder, and ground coriander. Mix well, then add the tomatoes and salt to taste. Cook for 5 minutes, stirring constantly. Stir in the tamarind water and water and slowly bring to a boil.

3 Lower the heat under the pan, then add the fish cubes and simmer for 5–6 minutes or until the fish is just cooked through.

4 Turn the heat as low as possible and pour in the coconut milk. Add the pepper. Simmer gently for 2 minutes, then remove the pan from the heat. Serve immediately with boiled rice or potatoes.

For a feast, this dry curried fish makes a fantastic combination with wetter chicken and meat dishes. It's crunchy and has a delicious spicy flavor. Serve it as a dry side dish or with plain rice or a green salad as a main dish. Pomfret or any flat fish can be used instead of sardines.

MEEN PORICHATHU

SHALLOW-FRIED MASALA SARDINES   **SOUTH INDIA**

serves 2-4
fragrant, spicy, and dry

4 sardines, about 10 oz
   (300 g) in total
5 tbsp vegetable oil
1 small onion, finely sliced
small handful of chopped
   cilantro leaves
wedges of lemon

Spice paste
1 onion, chopped
2 green chilies, chopped
½-in (1-cm) piece fresh ginger
   root, finely chopped
10 curry leaves
10 black peppercorns
½ tsp chili powder
½ tsp ground turmeric
2 tbsp wine or cider vinegar
1 tsp lemon juice
salt

1 Place all the ingredients for the spice paste in a food processor or blender. Process for 2–3 minutes to make a fine paste. Set aside.

2 Wash the fish under cold running water, then pat dry with paper towels. With a very sharp knife, make some slashes about 1 in (2.5 cm) apart along the whole length of the fish on both sides. Don't cut too deeply, just enough to break the skin and cut slightly into the flesh.

3 Place the fish on a baking sheet and spread the spice paste all over the fish, ensuring that it penetrates well into the cuts. Leave to marinate for 15–20 minutes.

4 Heat 2 tbsp of the oil in a large frying pan. Add the onion and cook for 5–6 minutes over very high heat until the onion is well browned and crisp. Remove the onion from the pan and drain on paper towels.

5 Heat the remaining oil in the same pan over low heat. Carefully place the fish in the pan, cover, and cook for about 6 minutes on each side. Turn the fish once only during cooking to avoid breaking it up. Cook until the skin is brown and the flesh is cooked through.

6 Carefully remove the fish and place on a large serving dish. Sprinkle the crisp onions over the fish and garnish with cilantro and lemon wedges.

In most of southern India, crabs are not often cooked at home, mainly because it is hard for cooks to prepare. Crab would more likely be prepared in homes in fishing communities or in the traditional toddy bars. Unlike the usual spicy dry preparation, for this curry, the crabs are cooked in a nicely spiced coconut milk sauce. Eat this with tamarind rice (p.148) or a bread such as chapatti or paratha.

NJANDU THENGAPAL

CRAB IN COCONUT MILK   **SOUTH INDIA**

serves 4
creamy and refreshing

3 tbsp vegetable oil
7 oz (200 g) shallots, finely
   sliced
10 curry leaves
3 garlic cloves, chopped
1-in (2.5-cm) piece fresh ginger
   root, finely sliced

½ tsp chili powder
½ tsp ground turmeric
1 fresh, uncooked crab, about
   14 oz (400 g), cleaned
   and quartered
1¼ cups coconut milk
2 tomatoes, quartered
salt
1 tsp lemon juice
½ tsp black pepper

1 Heat the oil in a large frying pan and fry the shallots for 5 minutes or until they are soft. Add the curry leaves, garlic, and ginger and cook for a further 5 minutes over medium heat.

2 Add the chili powder and turmeric, then slowly pour in 1 cup of water, stirring. Bring the mixture to a boil, then lower the heat and simmer for 10 minutes, stirring occasionally.

3 Add the crab pieces and continue simmering the curry over medium heat for 10 minutes or until the crab is cooked.

4 Stir in the coconut milk and tomatoes and heat through gently for 2–3 minutes. Add salt to taste. Remove the pan from the heat, cover, and set aside for a few minutes, then add the lemon juice and sprinkle with the black pepper. Serve immediately.

Jumbo shrimp dishes are a treat in coastal southern India, as shrimp are not easily affordable for ordinary people unless they live near beaches or areas where they can buy it fresh-caught. Kerala has its own distinctive ways of cooking shrimp and lobsters. This is a very popular dish in the local bars, which are well known for excellent spicy dishes. Eat this with breads like paratha, or plain rice.

KOYILANDI KONJU MASALA

BOATMAN'S SHRIMP MASALA   SOUTH INDIA

serves 4–6
vibrant and spicy

3 tbsp vegetable oil
pinch of cumin seeds
10 curry leaves
3 onions, sliced
½ tsp ground turmeric
1 tsp chili powder
1 tsp tomato paste

4 tomatoes, sliced
1-in (2.5-cm) piece fresh ginger
  root, thinly sliced
sea salt
1¼ lb (500 g) raw jumbo
  shrimp, peeled but last
  tail section left on
chopped cilantro leaves
  to garnish

1 Heat the oil in a large frying pan, *karahi*, or wok. Add the cumin seeds, curry leaves, and onions and cook over medium-low heat for 10 minutes, stirring occasionally, until the onions are golden.

2 Add the turmeric, chili powder, tomato paste, tomatoes, sliced ginger, and a little salt to taste. Cook for 5 minutes, stirring occasionally.

3 Add the shrimp and simmer for a further 5–6 minutes or until they turn pink and are just cooked.

4 Serve sprinkled with chopped cilantro leaves.

Pumpkins are festival vegetables in most of the states in southern India. They are grown abundantly in almost every household garden and cooked in all kinds of ways. There are many varieties, with a range of colors, flavors, sizes, and seasons. White pumpkin has a particularly delicious and refreshing flavor, which goes amazingly well with coconut and shrimp in this subtle curry. Serve with tamarind rice (p.148) or breads such as paratha.

KONJU PULUNGARI

JUMBO SHRIMP AND PUMPKIN CURRY   **SOUTH INDIA**

serves 4–6
subtle and light

2 tbsp vegetable oil
½ tsp mustard seeds
pinch of cumin seeds
10 curry leaves
1-in (2.5-cm) piece fresh ginger root, cut into strips
2 green chilies, slit lengthwise

2 onions, sliced
6 oz (150 g) peeled pumpkin flesh, thinly sliced
½ tsp ground turmeric
salt
1⅔ cups thick coconut milk
1¼ lb (500 g) raw jumbo shrimp, peeled but last tail section left on
1 tsp white vinegar

1 Heat the oil in a large frying pan. Add the mustard and cumin seeds, and when they start to pop, add the curry leaves, ginger, chilies, and onions. Cook over medium-low heat for 10 minutes, stirring occasionally, until the onions are golden.

2 Add the pumpkin, turmeric, and a little salt and mix well for 1 minute, then pour in the coconut milk and ¾ cup water. Bring the mixture to a boil, stirring constantly.

3 Add the shrimp to the pan and cook, stirring, for 5 minutes or until the shrimp and pumpkin are cooked. Add the vinegar and mix well. Serve hot with rice or bread.

Squid is enjoyed in both southern India and Sri Lanka, cooked as a curry, stuffed, or fried. If you go out on a boat to fish, the fishermen cook the freshly caught squid onboard with the minimum of spices and offer them as a special treat. Squid must be cooked for a short time or long simmered; otherwise, it will be rubbery. Try this with breads such as paratha or chapatti or any flavored rice.

KOONTHAL ULLATHIYATHU

SQUID CURRY   **SOUTH INDIA**

serves 4
warm and colorful

3 tbsp vegetable oil
½ tsp mustard seeds
2 large onions, sliced
3 green chilies, slit lengthwise
1-in (2.5-cm) piece fresh ginger root, finely sliced

½ tsp chili powder
½ tsp ground coriander
2 large tomatoes, sliced
14 oz (400 g) cleaned squid, cut into ½-in (1-cm) pieces and tentacles reserved
1 tbsp chopped cilantro leaves

1 Heat the oil in a large frying pan and add the mustard seeds. When they begin to pop, add the onions and cook for 5 minutes or until they are golden brown.

2 Stir in the green chilies and ginger, then add the chili powder and ground coriander. Mix well and add the tomatoes. Cook over medium heat for 5–10 minutes or until the tomatoes break down to give a thick sauce.

3 Add the squid pieces and tentacles and mix thoroughly. Cover and continue cooking over low heat for 15 minutes, stirring occasionally to prevent burning and sticking. If the dish becomes dry very quickly, stir in a few spoonfuls of water. Serve hot, garnished with the cilantro.

This delicious seafood preparation is from the Chettinad region of Tamil Nadu. Being ancient sea traders, the people of this region brought back recipes from other countries. They learned how to preserve food in dry form with spices for long voyages, which could be prepared as curries by adding water. Karuvapillai Yera is a shrimp preparation with traditional curry leaves and spices native to this region.

KARUVAPILLAI YERA

SHRIMP WITH SPICY CURRY LEAVES

SOUTH INDIA

serves 5
mildly spiced and velvety

15–17 raw shrimp, peeled and deveined
1 cup coconut oil
½ tsp fenugreek seeds
1 tbsp roughly crushed garlic
2 onions, finely chopped
2 sprigs of curry leaves
6 whole red chilies
1 tbsp ground coriander
5 medium-sized tomatoes, puréed
scant 1 oz (25 g) tamarind, made into pulp
3½ oz (100g) coconut paste

Marinade
1 tbsp ginger and garlic paste
1 tsp ground turmeric
2 tbsp lemon juice
salt

Dry mix
1¾ oz (50 g) split and husked black lentils (*urad dal*)
1¾ oz (50 g) split gram lentils (*chana dal*)
10 whole red chilies
15 sprigs of curry leaves
1 tbsp black peppercorns
1 tbsp cumin seeds

1 Mix all the ingredients for the marinade together with 2–3 tablespoons of water. Add the shrimp and turn to coat them, then cover and set aside for about 60 minutes.

2 Heat a wok or *kadhai* over medium heat and sauté all the ingredients for the dry mix until the lentils turn golden brown. Leave to cool, then transfer to a food processor and grind to a fine powder.

3 Coat the marinated shrimp with the dry lentil powder. Heat oil in a frying pan over medium heat and fry the shrimp until golden brown. Strain and set aside.

4 Add the fenugreek seeds, garlic, onions, and curry leaves to the oil and sauté for 1–2 minutes or until the onions turn golden. Add the red chilies and coriander, sprinkle 1 tablespoon of water, and sauté for another minute.

5 Fold in the tomato purée and cook for 3 minutes, stirring frequently. Mix in the tamarind pulp and add ½ cup water and cook for 2 minutes.

6 Reduce the heat to low, add the coconut paste along with ⅔ cup water, and cook for another 2 minutes, stirring continuously. Check the seasoning and add more salt if required. Add the shrimp and cook for a minute.

7 Serve the crispy shrimp gravy with steamed rice.

Oysters, in Western cuisine, are a French delicacy reserved for affluent clientele. However, this is a recipe from the erstwhile Chera kingdom, which was part of present-day Kerala and Coimbatore in the state of Tamil Nadu. This recipe is a modified version of the traditional one, with the addition of tomatoes.

ARIKOIDUKA THOKKU

OYSTERS COOKED IN TOMATO AND COCONUT   SOUTH INDIA

serves 5
mildly spiced and sour,
aromatic

25 fresh oysters, washed and cleaned
salt
1 tbsp lemon juice
1 tsp crushed black peppercorns
1 whole coconut, grated
3 tbsp vegetable oil
½ tsp mustard seeds
2 sprigs of curry leaves
½ tbsp chopped garlic
3 medium-sized shallots, finely chopped
2 cardamom pods

2 cloves
1 cinnamon stick, 1 in (2.5 cm) long
½ tbsp chopped ginger
¼ tsp ground turmeric
½ tsp red chili powder
1 tsp ground coriander
½ tsp ground cumin
¼ tsp ground garam masala
5 medium-sized tomatoes, finely chopped
½ tsp fennel seeds
scant 1 oz (25 g) split and husked black lentil (*urad dal*), roasted and finely powdered
4 green chilies, slit into halves
3 tbsp finely chopped cilantro leaves

1 Place the oysters in a large bowl and mix them with some salt, lemon juice, and half the crushed peppercorns. Set aside to marinate for 30 minutes.

2 Meanwhile, mix half of the grated coconut with a little water to make a paste. Roast the remaining grated coconut over medium heat until golden brown. Set aside.

3 Heat the oil in a heavy-bottomed saucepan over medium heat. Add the mustard seeds, half the curry leaves, and the garlic and sauté until the mustard seeds crackle and the garlic turns slightly brown. Add the shallots and sauté for a minute or until light brown. Stir in the cardamoms, cloves, cinnamon stick, and ginger and sauté

for 1 minute. Mix in the roasted coconut and sauté for another minute. The spices and grated coconut should cook well to blend together for flavor. Add the turmeric.

4 Add the oysters and sauté for 1 minute over medium heat. Mix in the chili powder, ground coriander, cumin, and garam masala. Add ⅔ water and cook for 2–3 minutes, stirring occasionally.

5 Add the tomatoes and fennel seeds and cook for 4–5 minutes. If necessary, add a tablespoon or two of water to prevent the masala from sticking to the bottom of the saucepan. Mix in the coconut paste and cook for 3–4 minutes, stirring occasionally. The coconut paste will thicken the gravy and enhance the taste. At this point, you may add a little more water if you do not want a thick gravy. This recipe keeps the gravy thick.

6 Add the roasted lentil powder and mix well. Once the oysters are cooked, add the chilies, salt, cilantro, and the remaining crushed peppercorns and curry leaves. Mix well and serve hot.

Balti is a cooking container similar to a wok in which the food is cooked. Balti curries are mostly semithin to thin gravies. People mostly cook mutton or chicken using this process, but this recipe is made with fish.

BALTI FISH CURRY

serves 5
aromatic and slightly spicy

2¼ lb (1 kg) sole or any other
  white fish fillet, cut into
  1½-in (4-cm) cubes
1¼ cups vegetable oil
1 tbsp grated ginger
1 tbsp roughly crushed garlic
3 medium-sized onions,
  finely chopped
1 tsp crushed coriander seeds
1 tsp red chili powder
½ tsp ground cumin
½ tsp ground turmeric

14 oz (400 g) tomatoes,
  finely chopped
3 oz (80 g) red pepper, diced
salt
⅔ cup coconut cream

Marinade
scant 1 oz (25 g) garlic cloves
1 tbsp lemon juice
salt

To garnish
1 tbsp chopped cilantro leaves
1 tsp chopped mint leaves

1 To prepare the marinade, peel the garlic and grind to a fine paste. Add a tablespoon or two of water and mix well. Pour the mixture into a piece of muslin. Gather the muslin and squeeze to extract the garlic juice. Mix the garlic juice with rest of the ingredients for the marinade. Add the cubes of fish and turn to coat them, then cover and set aside for 30 minutes.

2 Heat the oil in a *karahi* or wok over medium heat. Add the ginger and garlic and sauté for a minute or until light brown. Add the onions and sauté for 2–3 minutes or until translucent. Stir in the crushed coriander seeds, chili powder, cumin, and turmeric; mix well; and cook for another minute. Add the tomatoes and cook for 6–7 minutes, stirring frequently.

3 Lower the heat, add ¾ cup water, and cook the spice mix for 15 minutes. Add the red pepper, the marinated fish, and salt and simmer for 10 minutes.

4 Mix in the coconut cream and simmer for another 3–4 minutes or until the fish is cooked through.

5 Garnish with the cilantro and mint and serve hot with rice, *rogini naan*, or *roti*.

Shrimp (*jhinga*) are found abundantly in the warm waters of the Arabian Sea, which lies to the south of Pakistan. White-shelled shrimp, which are delicate in flavor, are the most common variety, followed by tiger shrimp. If available, use white-shelled shrimp for this curry, as they blend beautifully with the aromatic, spicy masala. The masala can be cooked in advance; however, the shrimp must be added and cooked just before serving. Cumin raita (p.180) and vegetable biryani (p.150) are good accompaniments.

JHINGA CURRY

SHRIMP CURRY   **PAKISTAN**

serves 4–5
fragrant and spicy

1¼ lb (500 g) raw jumbo or tiger shrimp
3 tbsp sunflower oil
1 onion, chopped
1 tsp garlic paste
1 tsp ginger paste
1 medium tomato, peeled and finely chopped
8 oz (225 g) plain Greek-style yogurt
1 tsp red chili powder
½ tsp ground black pepper
½ tsp ground turmeric
½ tsp cumin seeds
½ tsp ground coriander
salt
2 tbsp coarsely chopped green chilies
¼ cup chopped cilantro leaves
cilantro leaves to garnish

1 Peel the shrimp, leaving the last tail section on. Devein the shrimp, then set aside.

2 To make the masala, heat the oil in a saucepan, add the onion, and fry until light golden brown. Add the garlic and ginger pastes and stir for 1–2 minutes. Add the tomato and yogurt and cook, stirring, for another few minutes. Add the chili powder, black pepper, turmeric, cumin seeds, ground coriander, and salt to taste and cook, stirring, until the oil separates out.

3 Add the shrimp and cook over medium-high heat, stirring frequently, for 4–5 minutes or until the shrimp turn pink. Make sure you don't overcook them. Stir in the green chilies and chopped cilantro, and garnish with cilantro leaves. Serve hot.

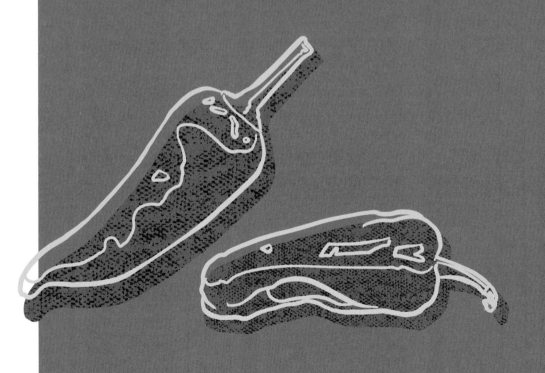

POULTRY

In Old Delhi in the 1950s, the legendary Moti Mahal restaurant created the dish that for millions of people around the world (especially in Britain) defines Indian food. "Butter Chicken," as Moti Mahal calls it, is the father and mother of chicken tikka masala. In the West, this dish is much interpreted, but in fact it has been enjoyed by Punjabis for decades. This is exactly how it is prepared in Old Delhi. Ideally, the chicken should be cooked in a *tandoor* on skewers to give a smoky flavor, but an oven or barbecue grill are good enough alternatives. The chicken should be cooked two-thirds of the way through and then simmered in the sauce. Collect the juices from the cooking chicken, strain, and add them to the sauce, too.

MURGH MAKHANI

OLD DELHI-STYLE CHICKEN CURRY   NORTH INDIA—DELHI & PUNJAB

serves 4–6
rich, smooth, and fragrant

1 tsp ginger paste
1 tsp garlic paste
1½ tsp salt
1½ tsp chili powder
juice of ½ lemon
1¾ lb (800 g) boned chicken
  thighs, skinned and cut in half
3½ oz (100 g) plain Greek-style
  yogurt
¼ tsp ground garam masala

Sauce
2¾ lb (1.25 kg) tomatoes,
  cut in half
1-in (2.5-cm) piece fresh ginger
  root, crushed

4 garlic cloves, peeled
4 green cardamom pods
2 cloves
1 cinnamon leaf or bay leaf
1½ tbsp Kashmiri chili powder
½ stick (¼ cup) butter, cut into
  small pieces
1-in (2.5-cm) piece fresh ginger
  root, finely chopped
2 green chilies, quartered
  lengthwise
⅓ cup heavy cream
1 tsp salt
1 tsp ground dried fenugreek
  leaves
¼ tsp ground garam masala
2 tsp sugar (optional)

1 Prepare the barbecue grill or preheat the oven to 450°F (220°C).

2 To make the marinade, mix together the ginger paste, garlic paste, salt, chili powder, and lemon juice in a large bowl. Add the chicken and, using your hands, coat the pieces with the mixture. Set aside for 20 minutes. Mix the yogurt with the garam masala and apply to the marinated chicken. Set aside for another 10 minutes if you have time.

3 Thread the chicken onto skewers. Cook on the barbecue grill or in the oven for 15–18 minutes, turning the skewers after 10 minutes or so, to cook evenly on both sides.

4 While the chicken is cooking, make the sauce. Place the tomatoes in a pan with ½ cup water and add the crushed ginger, garlic, cardamom pods, cloves, and cinnamon leaf. Cook until the tomatoes are completely broken down and soft.

5 Remove the pan from the heat and, using a hand-held blender, purée the mixture (or do this in a blender or food processor). Press through a sieve to make a very smooth purée.

6 Return the purée to the pan and bring to a boil. Stir in the chili powder. Cook until the purée starts to thicken, then slowly incorporate the butter, little by little, stirring constantly. The sauce will become glossy.

7 Add the chicken (off the skewers) and the strained juices from roasting. Simmer for 5–6 minutes. As the sauce begins to thicken, add the chopped ginger, green chilies, and cream. Continue simmering until the sauce is thick enough to coat the chicken.

8 Remove from the heat before the fat separates out and comes to the surface of the dish. (If that does happen, simply stir in 1–2 tbsp water and 1 tbsp more cream and remove immediately from the heat.) Add the salt, ground fenugreek, and garam masala and mix well. Check the seasoning and add the sugar, if needed.

9 Serve the chicken curry with hot *naan* (p.158) or pilau rice.

In the mid-18th century, competition between *rakabdars* (chefs) in Lucknow was at its peak. Each tried to outdo the others by creating ever more sophisticated dishes. Addition of gold leaf was, and still is, the ultimate luxurious adornment.

GUCCHI AUR MURGH KALIA

CHICKEN AND MOREL CURRY   **NORTH INDIA—LUCKNOW & AWADH**

serves 4–6
aromatic and spicy

1¾ oz (50 g) large dried morels
1 lb 2 oz (500 g) onions,
  finely sliced
vegetable oil for deep-frying
10 oz (300 g) plain yogurt
½ cup ghee or vegetable oil
1 tsp royal cumin seeds
1 tsp whole allspice
½ nutmeg
1 blade mace
4 green cardamom pods
½ tsp black peppercorns
2¼ lb (1 kg) boned chicken
  thighs, excess fat removed
  and each cut in half
  lengthwise

2 tbsp ginger paste
2 tbsp garlic paste
2 tbsp Kashmiri red chili
  powder
2 tsp salt
1 cup chicken stock
⅓ cup heavy cream
pinch of saffron threads
½ tsp ground garam masala
few drops of rosewater
  (optional)
2 sheets of gold leaf (optional)

1 Wash the morels thoroughly to get rid of any grit. Soak in ¾ cup water for 30 minutes to rehydrate. Drain the morels, reserving the liquid, and pat dry with paper towels.

2 While the morels are soaking, deep-fry the onions until golden. Drain, then blend with 1¾ oz (50 g) of the yogurt and a little water to make a paste.

3 Heat 1 tbsp of the ghee in a heavy-bottomed pan and add ½ tsp of the royal cumin. When it crackles, add the morels and sauté for a couple minutes over medium heat. Using a slotted spoon, remove the morels from the pan and set aside.

4 Heat the rest of the ghee in the pan and add the whole spices, together with the remaining royal cumin. Stir for 1–2 minutes, then add the chicken pieces. Saute for 2–3 minutes over high heat, then add the onion and the ginger and garlic pastes and mix together. Stir for another 2–3 minutes. Add the red chili powder and salt and cook for 2–3 minutes. Stir in the remaining yogurt, little by little. Cook for 5 minutes, then add the stock and the reserved morel soaking liquid. Reduce the heat, cover the pan, and simmer gently until the chicken is cooked.

5 Remove the chicken pieces with a slotted spoon and set aside. Pass the sauce through a sieve, then return to the pan and bring back to a boil. Boil until reduced to a saucelike consistency.

6 Reduce the heat to low and stir in the cream, saffron, and garam masala. Add the chicken pieces and simmer briefly to heat up. Lastly, just before serving, add the morels and finish with the rosewater, if using. Transfer to a shallow dish and garnish with the optional gold leaf.

The basic chicken curry differs from household to household. Every cook has their own recipe, and each swears by theirs. *Jhol* refers to the thin curry—or "gravy," as it's called in India—that makes it so special. This is quite a simple and rustic method of cooking—true home-style. You could use boneless chicken if you prefer, or even a whole bird cut up into small pieces. Or you could use quail, partridges, or even pheasants for this recipe; just adjust the cooking times.

MURGIR JHOL

HOME-STYLE CHICKEN CURRY   NORTH INDIA—BENGAL

serves 4-6
rustic, fresh, and spicy

⅓ cup corn or vegetable oil
½ tsp cumin seeds
2 cinnamon leaves or bay leaves
3 green cardamom pods
4 black peppercorns
4 large red onions, finely chopped
4 medium potatoes, peeled and cut into quarters (optional)
2 tsp salt
2¼ lb (1 kg) chicken thighs with bone, skinned and cut in half

1 tbsp ginger paste
1 tbsp garlic paste
2 tbsp ground coriander
2 tbsp ground cumin
1 tbsp chili powder
1 tbsp ground turmeric
4 tomatoes, chopped or blended to a purée
1⅔ cups chicken stock or water
3 green cardamom pods, roasted and ground
2-in (5-cm) cinnamon stick, roasted and ground
1 tbsp finely chopped cilantro leaves

1 Heat the oil in a large pan and add the whole spices. When they crackle, add the onions and fry over medium heat until golden brown. Stir in the potatoes, if using, and cook for 5 minutes. Add 1 tsp of the salt, then add the chicken and cook for 5–8 minutes or until lightly browned.

2 Add the ginger and garlic pastes, the ground coriander and cumin, remaining salt, chili powder, and turmeric. Cook for a further 10 minutes, stirring constantly, until the spices begin to release their aromas. Stir in the tomatoes and cook for 5 minutes, then pour in the stock. Bring to a boil. Reduce the heat to low and simmer until the chicken is cooked.

3 Taste and adjust the seasoning, if required. Top with the ground cardamom and cinnamon and finish with the chopped cilantro. Serve with steamed rice.

Mukul in Hindi refers to a flower bud. In this Rajasthani recipe, chicken pieces are cooked in special spices that render the pieces as soft as flower buds. Traditionally, royalty cooked it with game meat, such as rabbit, but it works equally well with chicken.

MURGH KE MUKUL

CREAMY CHICKEN CURRY NORTH INDIA

serves 5
mildly spiced and nutty

3 medium-sized onions, peeled
4 tbsp ghee
6 green cardamom pods
5 cloves
3 bay leaves
1 tbsp ginger and garlic paste (p.101)
½ tsp black peppercorns
½ tsp ground turmeric

1 tsp ground coriander
1 tsp red chili powder
1 tsp ground cumin
1 lb 5 oz (600 g) boneless chicken, julienned
1 cup yogurt, whisked until smooth
½ tsp nutmeg powder
½ tsp ground mace
salt
2 tbsp cashew nut paste
3 tbsp fresh cream

1 First, prepare the onion paste. Roughly chop 2 onions and boil them in ½ cup water for 5 minutes. Drain and leave to cool, then blend in a food processor to make a paste. Set aside.

2 Heat the ghee in a heavy-bottomed pan over medium heat. Add the cardamoms, cloves, and bay leaves and sauté for 30 seconds or until they release their flavor.

3 Finely chop the remaining onion and add to the spices. Sauté until golden. Stir in the ginger and garlic paste and sauté for another 30 seconds. Add in the peppercorns, turmeric, coriander, chili powder, and cumin powder and sauté for another 30 seconds. Reduce the heat to low; sprinkle a tablespoon or two of water; and cook, stirring frequently, until the oil separates.

4 Increase the temperate to medium-high, add the chicken, and sauté for 2 minutes. Mix in the onion paste and cook for 5 minutes, stirring frequently.

5 Fold in the yogurt and cook for another 5 minutes, stirring frequently. Add the nutmeg and mace and sprinkle in the salt. Reduce the heat to low, cover, and simmer for 7–9 minutes.

6 Uncover the pan and stir in the cashew nut paste, along with 1⅔ cups water. Cover and allow it to simmer for another 3 minutes or until the chicken is almost done.

7 Uncover the pan and fold in the cream. Add salt, if necessary. Discard the whole spices and serve this creamy chicken curry with rice or *roti*.

The term *shahjahani* suggests that this is a Mughlai preparation preferred by none other than Shah Jahan, the Mughal Emperor who built the Taj Mahal. However, over time with various adaptations, it became a popular dish in Awadhi cuisine. A garnish of saffron and omelet adds strength to this aromatic and rich curry.

CHICKEN SHAHJAHANI

NORTH INDIA

serves 5
rich and aromatic

2¼ lb (1 kg) boneless chicken breasts and legs, cleaned and cut into 20 pieces
2 tbsp ghee
5 green cardamom pods, crushed open
2 cinnamon sticks
5 cloves
3 bay leaves
2 medium-sized onions, chopped
5½ oz (150 g) plain yogurt, whisked
4 green chilies, finely chopped
¼ tsp grated nutmeg
¼ tsp ground mace
salt
¼ tsp ground cardamom
1 tbsp grated milk cheese
1 tbsp roasted and finely chopped golden raisins or raisins, to garnish
1 tbsp chopped cashew nuts, to garnish

Marinade
1 tbsp ginger and garlic paste
5 green chilies
½ tbsp lemon juice
3½ oz (100 g) plain yogurt, whisked
salt

Paste
1 tbsp poppy seeds
1¾ oz (50 g) cashew nuts
1½ oz (45 g) freshly grated coconut

Omelet
3 eggs
2 tbsp fresh cream
salt and freshly ground black peppercorns
pinch of saffron
1 tbsp vegetable oil

1 Mix together the ingredients for the marinade. Add the chicken pieces and toss to coat with the marinade, then cover and set aside for 30 minutes.

2 Meanwhile, blend the poppy seeds, cashew nuts, and grated coconut with 5 tablespoons of water in a food processor to make a paste.

3 Heat the ghee in a heavy-bottomed saucepan. Add the cardamoms, cinnamon stcks, cloves, and bay leaves and sauté for 10 seconds over medium heat. Add the onions and fry for 30 seconds or until translucent. Add the chicken along with the marinade and cook for 5 minutes, stirring occasionally. Cover the saucepan and let the chicken cook in its own juices. When almost dry, add the yogurt and mix well. Add the chilies and cover. Leave the chicken to cook for another 4–5 minutes or until almost tender.

4 Meanwhile, for the garnish, prepare the omelet by whisking together the eggs and cream. Season, add the saffron, and mix well. Heat the oil in a nonstick frying pan over medium heat. Pour the beaten egg into the pan and swirl to make a thin omelet. Cook for 3 minutes or until set. Transfer to a plate and cut into small pieces.

5 When the chicken is tender, add the paste and mix well. Sprinkle in the nutmeg and mace and cook for 2 minutes over medium heat. Add ⅔ cup water and stir. Add salt and cook for 5 minutes or until the chicken is cooked through. Sprinkle in the ground cardamom and milk cheese, mix well, and cook for another 30 seconds.

6 Transfer to a serving plate; remove the whole spices; and garnish with the omelet pieces, golden raisins, and cashew nuts.

Simple, mild chicken curries are typical of home cooking in the region, and Christian communities prepare chicken dishes for celebrations and special occasions, to be eaten with popular breads like *appams*. Home-reared chickens are preferred for their outstanding flavor.

KOZHY KURUMA

SOUTH INDIAN CHICKEN KORMA

SOUTH INDIA

serves 4
aromatic, nutty, and mild

3 tbsp vegetable oil
1-in (2.5-cm) cinnamon stick
3 cloves
2 bay leaves
3 cardamom pods, crushed
2 onions, chopped
1 tsp ground coriander
½ tsp ground turmeric
½ tsp chili powder
2 tsp tomato paste

1¼ lb (500 g) boneless, skinless chicken breast, cut into cubes
pinch of black pepper
salt
1¼ oz (40 g) cashew nuts, ground with a little water to make a paste
cilantro leaves to garnish

Ginger-garlic paste
1-in (2.5-cm) fresh ginger root, chopped
4 garlic cloves, peeled

1 For the ginger-garlic paste, put the ginger, garlic, and a little water in a small food processor or blender and grind to make fine paste. Set aside.

2 Heat the oil in a large frying pan. Add the cinnamon stick, cloves, bay leaves, and crushed cardamom pods and sauté for 2 minutes. Add the onions and stir well, then cook for 5 minutes or until the onions are soft.

3 Add the ginger-garlic paste, ground coriander, turmeric, chili powder, and tomato paste. Mix well, then cook over low heat for 5 minutes, stirring occasionally. Stir in the chicken, black pepper, salt to taste, and ⅔ cup water. Bring to a boil, then cover and simmer for 15–20 minutes or until the chicken is well cooked.

4 When the chicken is cooked, add the cashew paste and blend well. Simmer for a further 3 minutes. Serve hot, garnished with cilantro leaves.

Chicken curry is one of the highlights of weekend lunches in Sri Lanka. As in Keralan cooking, a special aroma is imparted with the use of coconut, and the layering of the spices makes it very easy to distinguish their various flavors. This dish comes from Colombo. Serve it with rice or bread.

KUKUL MUS KARI

SRI LANKAN CHICKEN CURRY

SRI LANKA

serves 4
very creamy and
  lightly spiced

3 tbsp vegetable oil
2 onions, finely sliced
1-in (2.5-cm) piece fresh ginger
  root, chopped
2 garlic cloves, chopped

½ tsp ground turmeric
1 tsp chili powder
2 tsp ground garam masala
14 oz (400 g) boneless,
  skinless chicken breast,
  cut into bite-sized pieces
¾ cup coconut milk
2 tomatoes, quartered
salt

1 Heat the oil in a medium saucepan, add the onions, and cook until golden brown. Add the ginger, garlic, and ground spices. Mix well for 1 minute, then add the chicken. Cook, stirring, over medium heat for 5 minutes.

2 Pour in 1¼ cups water. Bring to a boil, then reduce the heat, cover the pan, and cook for 10 minutes.

3 Turn the heat down very low and add the coconut milk. Cook for a further 10 minutes or until the chicken is cooked through. Stir in the tomatoes and salt to taste. Cook for a final 5 minutes to blend the masala well. Serve hot.

Generally, cooks prepare *istew*, the famous dish from South India, with vegetables or meat along with coconut milk, southern spices, and potatoes. Despite the distinctive flavor of the spices, the natural flavor of the main ingredients is not overpowered. The mild sweetness of the curry is from the freshly made coconut milk, which gives the dish its delicate flavor. People often eat *istew* with *appam*, *puttu*, or Malabar *paratha* for breakfast or brunch, and it is extremely light and healthy.

CHICKEN ISTEW

CHICKEN IN COCONUT MILK CURRY   SOUTH INDIA

serves 5
mildly sweet, delicately flavored

1 lb 2 oz (500 g) coconut, grated
2 tbsp coconut oil
½ tsp mustard seeds
5 green cardamom pods, roughly crushed
3 cloves
3 cinnamon sticks, each 1 in (2.5 cm) long
1 medium-sized onion, sliced
1 tsp roughly crushed ginger
½ tsp ground turmeric
2 sprigs of curry leaves
1 lb 10 oz–1¾ lb (750–800 g) skinless, bone-in chicken, cut into 18–20 pieces

1 medium-sized carrot, peeled and cut into ½-in (1-cm) cubes
6 green beans, ends trimmed and cut into ½-in (1-cm) pieces
2 medium-sized potatoes, peeled and cut in ½-in (1-cm) cubes
2 tbsp green peas
4 green chilies, slit open
salt
10 black peppercorns, roughly crushed
5–6 cashew nuts, ground with a little water to make a paste

1 To make the coconut milk, put the grated coconut along with ½ cup lukewarm water in a blender and process for 1–2 minutes to make a paste. Strain the paste through a fine strainer to extract the liquid, which will be thick coconut milk. Add another 1 cup water to the residue and grind into a fine paste. Once again, strain the paste through a fine strainer. You will now have thinner coconut milk.

2 In a heavy-bottomed saucepan, heat the oil over medium heat. Add the mustard seeds and allow them to crackle. Add the cardamoms, cloves, and cinnamon sticks and sauté for a minute or until they become slightly brown and roasted. Stir in the onion and ginger and fry for 1–2 minutes or until the onions turn soft and translucent but not brown. Add the turmeric and half of the curry leaves and sauté for 2 minutes.

3 Add the chicken pieces and cook for another 5 minutes or until the pieces start to acquire a light brown color. Pour in ⅔ cup water and the thin coconut milk. Cover the saucepan and cook for 17–20 minutes, stirring occasionally.

4 Remove the lid and add all the vegetables, along with ¾ cup water. Add the chilies and salt. Replace the lid and cook for another 3–4 minutes. Once the chicken and vegetables are tender, add the thick coconut milk and crushed peppercorns. Mix the cashew nut paste with the remaining curry leaves and add to the gravy. Cook for a minute, stirring constantly.

5 Remove the whole spices from the gravy and serve hot with *puttu*, *appam*, or steamed rice.

This dish comes from Tamil Nadu, where it is cooked for festivals like Diwali and other special occasions. In some of the villages, people prepare the dish as an offering to the goddess as part of worship. The spice combination and abundance of black pepper make this dish different from other Tamil chicken recipes. Enjoy its fiery savoriness and thick texture with Indian breads and a cold glass of beer.

KOLI ERACHI MOLAGU

CHICKEN PEPPER FRY

serves 4
peppery and thick

3 tbsp vegetable oil
½ tsp mustard seeds
10 curry leaves
1-in (2.5-cm) piece fresh ginger root, finely sliced
3 garlic cloves, chopped
3 green chilies, sliced
2 onions, chopped
2 tomatoes, diced
salt
1¼ lb (500 g) boneless, skinless chicken breasts, cut into ½-in (1-cm) cubes
large pinch of crushed black peppercorns

Spice paste

1 tbsp vegetable oil
4 oz (100 g) freshly grated coconut or desiccated coconut
2 cloves
2 cardamom pods
3 black peppercorns
½ in (1 cm) cinnamon stick
½ tsp chili powder
½ tsp ground turmeric
1 tsp ground coriander

1 To make the spice paste, heat the oil in a frying pan and roast the coconut with the cloves, cardamom pods, peppercorns, and cinnamon stick until the coconut is brown. Add the ground spices and sauté for 1 minute. Leave to cool, then transfer to a food processor or blender. Add ¾ cup water and grind to make a fine paste. Set aside.

2 Heat the oil in a large saucepan and add the mustard seeds. As they begin to pop, add the curry leaves, ginger, garlic, and green chilies. Cook for 3 minutes. Add the onions and cook until they are golden brown. Add the tomatoes and cook for another minute, then pour in the spice paste and add some salt. Stir well.

3 Add the chicken cubes and 1 cup of water. Bring to a boil, then cover the pan and cook for 20 minutes or until the chicken is cooked. Serve hot, sprinkled with the black pepper.

In the 1950s and '60s, if you were invited to dinner and served this curry, it would show that your hosts had spared no expense or effort in your honor, and you would have been duly thankful. Thus was the status of a "Desi Murgh" curry, when chickens were hard to obtain, very expensive, and difficult to cook. Farmed chicken changed all this and turned a glorious curry into an ordinary one. To get the real taste of the original, you have to use a *desi murgh*—a young, male, organic pasture-raised chicken. It should be slowly cooked until tender to allow all the herbs and spices to penetrate and release the full flavor of the chicken. If necessary, you can use a regular chicken instead of a free-range organic bird; however, you will probably need to reduce the amount of water for cooking. Serve with mango pickle (p.179) and *naans* or boiled or pulao rice.

DESI MURGH CURRY

SPECIAL CHICKEN CURRY   PAKISTAN

serves 4
spicy and flavorful

¼ cup sunflower oil
2 large onions, finely sliced
2 tsp garlic paste
2 tsp ginger paste
4 tomatoes, peeled and finely chopped
2 oz (50 g) plain Greek-style yogurt
1½ tsp red chili powder
1 tsp ground turmeric

1 tsp cumin seeds
2 tsp ground coriander
3 large black cardamom pods
6 cloves
1 bay leaf
salt to taste
1 pasture-raised organic chicken, about 2¾ lb (1.2 kg), cut into 8 pieces, skinned if preferred
5–6 tbsp chopped cilantro leaves

1 Heat the oil in a large saucepan, add the onions, and cook until dark golden brown. Remove the onions with a slotted spoon. Allow to cool, then chop them finely in a food processor. Set aside.

2 Add the garlic and ginger pastes to the hot oil in the saucepan and stir for a few minutes. Add the tomatoes and stir in well, then stir in the yogurt. Cook for 5–6 minutes. Add the browned onion paste and stir to mix, then add all the spices, the bay leaf, and salt to taste. Cook, stirring, until the oil separates out.

3 Put the chicken pieces in the pan and spoon the spice mixture over them. Add 2 cups water. Put the lid on the pan and cook over low heat, stirring occasionally, for 40–50 minutes or until the chicken is cooked through and tender. Add more water if needed.

4 Remove the lid and continue cooking for 10 minutes or until the oil in the sauce separates out. Stir in ¼ cup of the chopped cilantro. Garnish with the remaining chopped cilantro and serve.

Note You can make this curry in advance and reheat it in the pan on low heat or in a microwave.

In the 1750s, when *bawarchis* (cooks) supplied prepared dishes to their wealthy patrons, the food was delivered in covered and sealed trays to prevent any tampering. A dish such as this would have been cooked for special occasions. Served with a pilau, it could be the centerpiece of your dinner table. Other game birds such as partridge, pheasant, or grouse will also work well.

BATAIR MASALA

QUAIL IN SPICY CURRY

NORTH INDIA—LUCKNOW & AWADH

serves 6
slightly fatty and aromatic

6 quail, about 10 oz (300 g) each, skinned
scant 1 oz (25 g) ginger paste
scant 1 oz (25 g) garlic paste
2½ tsp red chili powder
1 tsp ground turmeric
2½ tsp salt
¾ cup vegetable oil or ghee
1-in (2.5-cm) cinnamon stick
1 blade mace

2 black cardamom pods
1 tbsp black peppercorns
5 cloves
5 green cardamom pods
9 oz (250 g) onions, processed to a fine paste
2 tbsp ground coriander
1 lb (450 g) plain yogurt
1½ tbsp chickpea flour
1 tsp ground garam masala
⅓ cup finely chopped cilantro leaves

1 Clean the quail inside and out by washing under cold running water; drain and pat dry using paper towels. Season them by rubbing with a mixture of 1 tbsp ginger paste, 1 tbsp garlic paste, 1 tsp red chili powder, ½ tsp turmeric, and 1 tsp salt. Set aside to marinate for 10–15 minutes.

2 Choose a shallow but wide pan that can hold the quail in it comfortably and has a tight-fitting lid. Set the pan over medium heat and pour in the oil. When hot, place the quail in the pan, a few at a time, and cook until they are golden brown on all sides. Using a slotted spoon, transfer the quail to a dish and set aside.

3 Heat the juices and oil left in the pot and add the whole spices, stirring to release their aromas. Add the onion paste and the remainder of the ginger and garlic pastes and cook, stirring constantly to prevent the pastes from sticking to the bottom of the pan. After 5–6 minutes, add the remainder of the chili powder, turmeric, and salt and the ground coriander. Cook until the fat begins to separate out from the pastes.

4 Return the seared quail to the pot and spoon the sauce over them carefully, taking care not to break the birds. Whisk the yogurt with the chickpea flour, then pour over the birds and mix into the sauce. Cover with the lid, reduce the heat to low, and cook for 15–20 minutes.

5 Remove the lid and transfer the quail to a serving dish; keep warm. Whisk the sauce for a few minutes using a hand whisk or fork to emulsify the mixture. It will still separate a little but should have a coating consistency. Taste and adjust the seasoning if required and finish with the garam masala and fresh cilantro. Spoon the sauce over the quail and serve immediately.

Until a few years ago, quail (*batair*) were only available as wild game and were considered a great delicacy, deemed fit only for *nawabs* and *maharajas*. Now, however, quail are farmed and easily available to everyone. This combination of quail and yogurt is ideal, as the yogurt tenderizes the birds and the tartness highlights their flavor. Other game birds like partridges can be cooked in the same way—use 6 partridges and increase the cooking time slightly. Serve with fresh cilantro chutney (p.178) and chickpea pilau (p.149) or *naans*.

BATAIR DAHI WALA

QUAIL IN YOGURT CURRY   PAKISTAN

serves 4
light and gamy

¼ cup sunflower oil
1 large onion, finely sliced
salt
12 red chilies
½ tsp red chili powder
2 cinnamon sticks
4 black cardamom pods

8 cloves
20 black peppercorns
2 bay leaves
1 tsp cumin seeds
12 quail, about 3 oz (75 g) each, skinned if preferred
10 oz (300 g) plain Greek-style yogurt
cilantro leaves to garnish

1 Heat the oil in a large saucepan, add the sliced onion, and cook until lightly golden brown. Add some salt, the whole chilies, and all the spices and stir for a few minutes. Add the quail and stir for a few more minutes to be sure they are well coated with the spice mixture.

2 Add the yogurt and stir to mix, then reduce the heat to medium-low and cook, uncovered, for 20–25 minutes, stirring occasionally.

3 With the tip of a sharp knife, check that the quail are fully cooked and tender, then continue stirring gently until all excess liquid has evaporated and the oil separates out. Garnish with cilantro leaves and serve.

NOTE You can make this curry in advance and reheat it in the pan over low heat or in a microwave.

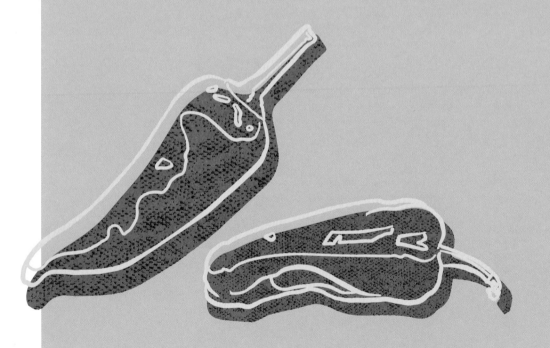

MEAT

As the name suggests, this is a very hot dish that is not for people with a weak constitution. It is by far the hottest dish in this chapter and is one of the few Indian dishes that contains heat in every sense—both "chili hot" and "spice hot." You can decide the amount of heat you'd like in your finished dish—discard most of the seeds from the chilies if you want to reduce the heat, or keep them in if you want it really hot. I think this is perfect for cold winter evenings or even a Friday night gathering. You can use either lamb or goat—they are interchangeable.

LAAL MAAS

FIERY LAMB CURRY   **NORTH INDIA—RAJASTHAN**

serves 4
chili hot

25–35 dried red chilies, stems removed
1½ tsp cloves
5½ oz (150 g) ghee or vegetable oil
9 oz (250 g) plain yogurt, whisked until smooth
2 tsp cumin seeds, roasted
1½ tbsp ground coriander
1 tsp red chili powder
2 tsp salt

3 cinnamon leaves or bay leaves
6 green cardamom pods
5 black cardamom pods
2½ oz (75 g) garlic cloves, finely chopped
9 oz (250 g) onions, finely chopped
2¼ lb (1 kg) leg of lamb or goat with bone, chopped into 1-in (2.5-cm) cubes
3 cups lamb stock or water
2 tbsp finely chopped cilantro leaves

1 Set aside 3 or 4 of the dried chilies to use later; put the remainder to soak in ½ cup water. Also put aside 4–6 of the cloves and 1 tbsp of the ghee.

2 Mix the yogurt with the cumin seeds, ground coriander, chili powder, and salt in a bowl. Set aside.

3 Heat the rest of the ghee in a heavy-bottomed pan. Add the remaining cloves, the cinnamon leaves, and the green and black cardamoms. When they begin to crackle and change color, add the garlic. Sauté for 2 minutes or until the garlic begins to turn golden. Add the onions and cook for 10 minutes or until golden brown, stirring constantly.

4 Stir in the meat and cook for 2–3 minutes. Drain the soaked red chilies and add to the pan. Continue cooking for 10–12 minutes or until the liquid has evaporated and the meat starts to brown slightly. Now add the spiced yogurt and cook for another 10–12 minutes or until the liquid from the yogurt has evaporated.

5 Add the stock or water and bring to a boil, then cover the pan, reduce the heat, and simmer until the meat is tender. Adjust the seasoning. Remove from the heat and keep warm.

6 To prepare the *tadka*, or tempering, which boosts the flavors, heat up the reserved ghee or oil in a large ladle over a flame (or in a small pan) and add the reserved cloves and dried red chilies. Cook for 1–2 minutes or until the ghee changes color and the spice flavors are released. Pour the contents of the ladle over the lamb curry, sprinkle with the chopped cilantro, and serve.

This is a true example of regional Indian cooking using local ingredients to make a dish that is not only unique but also appropriate for the region. The climate in most of Rajasthan and the Thar Desert is arid, and, while not a lot is produced here, corn is grown and consumed in abundance. Sweet corn helps water retention in the body, and yogurt is also cooling in a hot climate. This recipe uses lamb, but it would work just as well with goat or mutton, if you can get some.

MAKAI KA SOWETA

LAMB AND SWEET CORN CURRY   **NORTH INDIA—RAJASTHAN**

serves 4–6
warmly spiced

2¼ lb (1 kg) boned shoulder
    of lamb, cut into
    1-in (2.5-cm) cubes
½ cup ghee or corn oil
1½ tsp cumin seeds
5 green cardamom pods
4 black cardamom pods
10 cloves
2 cinnamon leaves or
    bay leaves
3 cups lamb stock or water
1 lb (450 g) canned sweet
    corn, drained and coarsely
    chopped
juice of ½ lemon
2 tbsp chopped cilantro
    leaves

Marinade
10 oz (300 g) plain yogurt
2 tsp ground coriander
1 tsp ground turmeric
2 tsp salt

Onion paste
7 oz (200 g) onions, finely
    chopped
3 oz (75 g) garlic cloves,
    finely chopped
12 green chilies

1 Mix together the ingredients for the marinade. Add the cubes of lamb and turn to coat, then cover and set aside for about 15 minutes.

2 Meanwhile, make the onion paste by blending together the ingredients in a blender until smooth.

3 Heat the ghee in a heavy-bottomed pan over medium heat, then add all the spices and the cinnamon or bay leaves. As the spices crackle, add the marinated cubes of lamb, with the marinade, and turn up the heat to high. Cook for 12–15 minutes or until all the moisture has evaporated, stirring constantly.

4 Next, add the onion paste and cook for a further 10 minutes, still stirring to ensure that the paste does not stick to the pan and burn. Add the lamb stock and reduce the heat. Simmer for 30 minutes or until the meat is about 85 percent cooked.

5 Add the sweet corn and cook for another 10 minutes, stirring constantly. The dish is ready when the consistency is glossy. Remove from the heat, adjust the seasoning, and transfer to a heated serving dish. Finish with the lemon juice and fresh cilantro. Serve with steamed rice or bread.

This is a very simple dish to make but is a great indicator of the level of finesse and sophistication in cooking that was reached during the reign of certain Mughal rulers in Lucknow. Slow cooking gives a unique shine and smoothness to the sauce from the gelatin in the lamb.

NALLI GOSHT

SLOW-BRAISED LAMB SHANK IN SAFFRON SAUCE   **NORTH INDIA—LUCKNOW & AWADH**

serves 4
smooth and warmly spiced

4 lamb shanks
3 tbsp corn oil
2 black cardamom pods, crushed
2 cinnamon sticks
2 large onions, finely chopped
1 tsp ginger paste
1 tsp garlic paste
1½ tsp chili powder
½ tsp ground fennel seeds
½ tsp ground coriander
1 tsp ground ginger
2 tbsp plain yogurt
5 tomatoes, puréed
1½ tsp salt
2½ cups lamb stock or water

To finish
¼ tsp ground garam masala
generous pinch of saffron threads
3 drops of rosewater (optional)
2 tbsp heavy cream

1 First, blanch the lamb shanks: place them in a large saucepan of boiling water, cover, and cook for 20 minutes. Drain. When cool enough to handle, cut away all the gristle from the meat.

2 Heat the oil in a pan large enough to hold the shanks. Add the cardamom pods and cinnamon sticks, and when they crackle, add the onions. Cook until golden brown. Add the ginger and garlic pastes and cook for 2 minutes, stirring constantly. Add the ground spices and cook for 3 more minutes.

3 Slowly whisk in the yogurt and stir until the sauce reaches simmering point. Stir in the fresh tomato purée and bring the sauce to a boil. Season with the salt.

4 Add the lamb shanks to the simmering sauce. Cover with a tight-fitting lid and cook over low heat for 1½–2 hours or until the lamb is very tender and the meat is almost falling off the bone. Add some stock from time to time; you will need the extra liquid to cook the shanks completely.

5 Alternatively, you can cook the lamb shanks in the oven. Put them in a braising tray, cover with the sauce and stock, and braise in a preheated 350°F (180°C) oven for 2½–3 hours. Keep checking the shanks after 2 hours.

6 Remove the shanks and arrange them on a serving tray or plate. Cover and keep warm in a warm oven while you finish the sauce.

7 Skim any excess fat or oil from the sauce, then strain the sauce into a smaller saucepan and return to the heat. Add the garam masala powder, saffron, and rosewater, if using. Bring to a boil again, adjust the seasoning, and stir in the cream. Remove the shanks from the oven and pour the sauce over them. Serve immediately.

This recipe has its origins in Kashmir, the northernmost state of India, on the border of Pakistan, where the winters are severe. This is a simple yet warming everyday dish using turnips, carrots, spinach, and dill with lamb. It could have been the starting point of what the Western world knows as *saag gosht* minus the root vegetables, but try it with the vegetables and see the difference for yourself.

SUBZ SAAG GOSHT

LAMB COOKED WITH WINTER VEGETABLES AND SPINACH · NORTH INDIA—DELHI & PUNJAB

serves 4
rich, spicy, and rustic

⅓ cup ghee or corn oil
2 tsp cumin seeds
2 tsp cloves
2 large onions, finely chopped
1¾ oz (50 g) garlic, finely chopped
1½ oz (40 g) fresh ginger root, finely chopped
2 tsp red chili powder
1 tsp ground turmeric
2 tsp salt
2¼ lb (1 kg) boned leg of lamb, cut into 1-in (2.5-cm) cubes

4 green chilies, slit lengthwise
5½ oz (150 g) each turnips and carrots, cut into ½-in (1-cm) cubes
1¼ cups lamb stock or water
7 oz (200 g) tomatoes, finely chopped
14 oz (400 g) spinach leaves, finely chopped
1½ tsp ground mixed spices (equal parts cloves, nutmeg, mace, and green cardamom)
2 tbsp finely chopped fresh dill leaves

1 Heat the ghee or oil in a large, heavy pan and add the cumin seeds and cloves. When they crackle, add the onions and sauté until they become light golden in color. Add the garlic and ginger and sauté for a further 2–3 minutes or until the garlic begins to change color.

2 Sprinkle in the red chili powder, turmeric, and salt and stir for another couple of minutes until the spices begin to release their aromas and the fat starts to separate out. Now add the cubes of lamb and cook for 5–6 minutes, stirring constantly, until the lamb begins to brown around the edges.

3 When most of the liquid has evaporated and the lamb is getting browned, add the green chilies and the turnips and carrots and stir. Pour in the lamb stock. Reduce the heat to low, cover with a lid, and cook until the lamb is three-quarters done.

4 Remove the lid, add the tomatoes, and cook for a further 10–12 minutes or until the lamb is nearly cooked and the tomatoes are incorporated with the masala. Stir in the spinach and increase the heat again. Cook for 2–3 minutes. (You can cover with a lid if you wish to speed up the cooking of the spinach.)

5 The lamb and spinach should be cooked by now, so check for seasoning and correct if required. To finish the dish, sprinkle with the ground mixed spices and dill, then cover the pan with the lid and remove from heat.

6 Remove the lid from the pan at the table and serve immediately, with chapatti or tandoori roti.

Shoulder of lamb is very good for braising, which is one of the cooking techniques used to make this dish. It is similar to a North Indian *korma*, but it has a sharp kick and freshness from the green chilies and mint, as well as a great texture resulting from adding onions and more chilies at the end.

KACHHI MIRCH KA GOSHT

LAMB SHOULDER WITH GREEN CHILIES, MINT, AND YOGURT   NORTH INDIA—LUCKNOW & AWADH

serves 4
sharp, hot, and fresh

2¼ lb (1 kg) boned shoulder of lamb, cut into 1½-in (3.5-cm) cubes
10 oz (300 g) plain yogurt
1½ tsp black peppercorns, coarsely crushed
2 tsp coriander seeds, roasted and coarsely pounded
2 tsp cumin seeds, roasted and coarsely pounded
2 tsp salt
⅓ cup ghee or corn oil
1 blade mace
5 black cardamom pods

9 oz (250 g) white onions, finely chopped
¾ oz (20 g) fresh ginger root, finely chopped
6 green chilies, slit lengthwise
3 cups lamb stock or water
1½ oz (40 g) cashew nut paste
2½ tbsp heavy cream
1 red onion, cut into ½-in (1-cm) cubes
1 tbsp finely chopped mint leaves
juice of 1 lemon
1 tsp ground roasted fennel seeds

1 Wash the diced lamb in cold running water for 10 minutes to remove any blood. Dry using paper towels. Put the lamb in a bowl with the yogurt, peppercorns, roasted and pounded coriander and cumin, and salt. Toss to mix, then set aside to marinate.

2 Reserve 1 tbsp of the ghee for later use and heat the rest in a heavy-bottomed pan. Add the mace and black cardamoms and stir for a few seconds. Add the white onions and cook them over medium heat until soft and translucent but not brown. As they begin to turn slightly golden, add the ginger and 4 of the green chilies.

3 Add the marinated lamb and stir. Cook for 12–15 minutes, stirring constantly, making sure that the lamb does not brown in the process. Pour in the stock, reduce to low heat, and cook, covered, until the lamb is almost done.

4 Stir in the cashew nut paste and cook for a further 5–7 minutes. Add the cream and adjust the seasoning, if required. Leave to simmer gently.

5 In a separate pan, heat the remaining ghee and briskly sauté the red onion and the remaining green chilies until the onion is soft and translucent. Add to the simmering lamb, sprinkle on the mint and lemon juice, and stir in the fennel powder. Serve immediately, with paratha (p.154) or pilau.

This is a lamb curry from West Bengal and is quite popular in Bihar and neighboring areas as well. The term *kosha* literally translated means "tightened," which refers to the thickening of the spices and sauce to give a rich finish. The curry is often served on a cold day with a soft *khichri*, the original kedgeree, the combination being both comforting and invigorating.

KOSHA MANGSHO

LAMB COOKED IN RICH ONION SAUCE

NORTH INDIA—BENGAL

serves 4
rich, spicy, and slightly sweet

3½ tbsp mustard oil
3½ tbsp ghee or vegetable oil
3 cinnamon leaves or bay leaves
5 black peppercorns
3 black cardamom pods
4 dried red chilies
3 blades mace
6 large red onions, blended to a paste
2 heaped tbsp ginger paste
2 heaped tbsp garlic paste
¼ cup red chili powder

2 tbsp ground cumin
2 tbsp ground coriander
2¼ lb (1 kg) boned leg of lamb, cut into 1-in (2.5-cm) cubes
5 large tomatoes, puréed
1½ tbsp salt
1⅔ cups lamb stock or water
1 tsp caster sugar

To finish
2 tsp each cinnamon stick, green cardamom pods, and coriander seeds, roasted and ground to a powder (p.173)
finely chopped cilantro leaves

1 Heat the mustard oil in a deep pan and bring to smoking point, then add the ghee, followed by the whole spices. When they start to crackle, stir in the onion paste and fry until it is light brown, stirring constantly to prevent it from sticking to the bottom of the pan and burning.

2 Add the ginger and garlic pastes and mix into the onions along with the chili powder and ground cumin and coriander. Fry for 2–3 minutes, then add the cubes of lamb. Cook over medium heat for 15–20 minutes, stirring frequently.

3 Add the puréed tomatoes and salt and cook for a further 15 minutes. Pour in the stock, reduce the heat to low, and cover the pan. Simmer until the lamb is tender. Uncover the pan, increase the heat, and reduce the sauce until it becomes thick and coats the lamb.

4 Adjust the seasoning with salt, if required, and stir in the sugar to balance the spiciness of the dish. Finally, stir in the ground roasted spices and sprinkle generously with chopped cilantro. Serve immediately with paratha (p.154), or even with a kedgeree.

Yakhni is a traditional dish of the Kashmiri *wazwan*, a multicourse meal in Kashmiri cuisine. This is an exotic yet simple, authentic Indian lamb or goat curry cooked in yogurt and milk gravy with aniseed and ginger powder. This aromatic curry is generally served with steamed rice or pilau.

GOSHT YAKHNI

MUTTON IN YOGURT CURRY   NORTH INDIA

serves 5
mildly spiced and aromatic

2¼ lb (1 kg) mutton, bones reserved, washed, dried, and cut into 1½-in (4-cm) cubes
1 tsp ginger and garlic paste
3 cinnamon sticks, each 2 in (5 cm) long
7 black cardamom pods
1 tbsp ground aniseed
1½ tsp ground cumin
10 oz (300 g) plain yogurt

1 oz (30 g) milk cheese (*khoya*), grated
½ tbsp sugar
12 green cardamom pods, crushed
1 tbsp ground dried ginger
salt
1 cup whole milk
3 tbsp ghee
1 tsp chopped cilantro leaves (optional)
1 tsp chopped mint leaves (optional)

1 Place the mutton in a heavy-bottomed casserole dish and add the ginger and garlic paste, cinnamon sticks, black cardamom pods, ground aniseed, and ground cumin, along with 3 cups water.

2 Place the casserole over medium heat, cover, and cook for 30 minutes, stirring occasionally. If the water is drying up, add another ½ cup water. Once the meat is three-quarters cooked, reduce the heat and allow it to simmer. (Check to see if the meat is cooked by piercing a mutton piece with a fork. If the piece starts to break but does not fall apart, it is three-quarters cooked.)

3 Meanwhile, in a separate bowl, mix together the yogurt, milk cheese, sugar, green cardamom pods, ground dried ginger, and salt. Add the mixture to the meat, stir for 2 minutes, cover, and simmer for another 10 minutes. As the gravy starts acquiring a slightly thick consistency, add the milk, stirring continuously to prevent it from curdling. Simmer for another 8–10 minutes and check the seasoning.

4 Add the ghee, stir, and cook for another 2–3 minutes. Garnish with cilantro and mint leaves, if using, and serve hot.

Hyderabad is known for its spicy meat and chicken dishes, and even more for its meat biryanis. The traditional Islamic community there has introduced lots of new cooking combinations and delicacies to modern Indian cuisine. Mutton is the favorite meat. This dish was once called a royal dish and enjoyed only by rich people, but today it is found on Indian restaurant menus all over the world. Serve with tamarind rice (p.148) or chapattis.

ATTIRACHI KOOT

HYDERABADI MUTTON   SOUTH INDIA

serves 4
spicy

1¼ lb (500 g) boned mutton, cut into ½-in (1-cm) cubes
¼ cup vegetable oil
2 cloves
2 cardamom pods
½-in (1-cm) piece of cinnamon stick
1 bay leaf
1 onion, finely chopped
salt
cilantro leaves to garnish

Marinade
1 tsp ginger paste
1 tsp garlic paste
2 tomatoes, finely chopped
1 onion, finely chopped
½ tsp ground turmeric
½ tsp chili powder
1 tsp ground coriander
2 tbsp cilantro leaves

1 Mix together the ingredients for the marinade in a bowl. Add the cubes of mutton and toss to coat with the marinade. Set aside for 20 minutes.

2 Heat the oil in a large saucepan and add the cloves, cardamom pods, cinnamon stick, and bay leaf. Sauté for 1 minute, then add the onion and cook until it is golden.

3 Add the marinated mutton to the pan with salt to taste and mix well. Cover and cook over low heat for about 30 minutes or until the mutton is tender. Garnish with cilantro leaves and serve.

Lamb dishes are very popular with Keralans, and they like to experiment by adding unusual ingredients like plantain. Lamb is an expensive meat for home cooks, so this is a dish for special occasions. Breads like chapatti and paratha (p.154) are good with it.

ETHAKKA ATTIRACHI CURRY

LAMB AND PLANTAIN CURRY   **SOUTH INDIA**

serves 4
spicy and rich

¼ cup vegetable oil
1 tsp mustard seeds
10 curry leaves
1-in (2.5-cm) piece fresh ginger root, chopped
5 garlic cloves, chopped
2 green chilies, chopped

2 onions, sliced
2 tsp ground coriander
½ tsp ground turmeric
½ tsp chili powder
3 tomatoes, sliced
14 oz (400 g) boned lamb, cut into cubes
1 plantain, peeled and cut into small pieces
salt

1 Heat the oil in a large frying pan. Add the mustard seeds and, when they start to pop, add the curry leaves. Then add the ginger, garlic, and green chilies and sauté for 3 minutes. Add the onions and cook for a further 10 minutes or until the onions are brown.

2 Stir in the ground coriander, turmeric, chili powder, and tomatoes, mixing well, then add the lamb and 1⅔ cups water. Bring to a boil, then cover and cook over low heat for 15 minutes.

3 Now stir in the plantain pieces along with some salt. Leave to cook for another 15 minutes or until the lamb is cooked through and the plantain is tender, stirring occasionally. Serve hot.

This is a restaurant specialty, famously known as Malabar mutton curry, cooked all over southern India in Malabari restaurants. Muslims in Calicut are very fond of this dish, as it is easy to cook and has an extraordinary taste. The roasted coconut base and peppercorn flavor are typical of Keralan cooking. Plain rice or paratha (p.154) are the best accompaniments.

KERALA LAMB

serves 4
exquisite and aromatic

3 tbsp vegetable oil
7 oz (200 g) shallots, chopped
1 tbsp ground coriander
½ tsp ground turmeric
½ tsp chili powder
salt
1¼ lb (500 g) boned lamb,
    cut into cubes

Spice paste

4 oz (100 g) freshly grated
    coconut or desiccated
    coconut
1-in (2.5-cm) piece fresh ginger
    root, sliced
3 garlic cloves, chopped
1-in (2.5-cm) cinnamon stick
3 cloves
2 bay leaves
10 curry leaves
5 black peppercorns

For tempering
2 tbsp vegetable oil
½ tsp mustard seeds
10 curry leaves
2 green chilies, slit lengthwise

1 First, make the spice paste. Roast the coconut with the ginger, garlic, cinnamon stick, cloves, bay leaves, curry leaves, and peppercorns in a dry pan until the coconut is browned. Allow to cool, then grind in a food processor, gradually adding about 1 cup water to make a fine paste.

2 Heat the 3 tbsp of oil in a frying pan, add the shallots, and fry for 5 minutes or until soft. Add the spice paste, the ground coriander, turmeric, chili powder, some salt, and 1⅔ cups of water. Bring to a boil. Add the lamb, then reduce the heat and cook, covered, for 30 minutes or until the lamb is well cooked.

3 Now prepare the tempering mixture. In a separate frying pan, heat the oil and add the mustard seeds. Once they start popping, add the curry leaves and green chilies. Stir-fry for 1 minute.

4 Pour the tempering mixture over the lamb curry and continue cooking for about 10 minutes or until the curry is very dry and thick. Serve hot.

This recipe from Hyderabad is a tantalizing concoction of *chana* and *toor dal*, cooked with mutton and spices to give a mildly sour but rich curry. Gosht Dalcha is often served as an accompaniment for biryani.

GOSHT DALCHA

MUTTON IN LENTIL CURRY

SOUTH INDIA

serves 5
mildly sour and aromatic

4 tbsp vegetable oil
6 green cardamom pods
6 cloves
4 cinnamon sticks, 2 in (5 cm) each
½ tsp cumin seeds
½ tsp ground turmeric
3 medium-sized onions, sliced
1 oz (30 g) split gram lentils (*chana dal*)
1 oz (30 g) split yellow lentils (*toor dal*)
1 tbsp ginger and garlic paste
½ tbsp red chili powder
½ tbsp ground coriander
1 lb 2 oz (500 g) neck end of mutton, washed and cleaned
1¾ oz (50 g) each of eggplant, potatoes, and pumpkins, each washed and sliced into 2-in (5-cm) long and ½-in (1-cm) wide strips
1 medium-sized raw mango
½ tsp ground garam masala

3½ oz (100 g) mildly sour yogurt
salt

Stock
1 lb 2 oz (500 g) mutton neck bones, washed and cleaned
1 medium-sized onion, sliced
4 garlic cloves
2 bay leaves
scant 1 oz (25 g) ginger, crushed
¼ tsp crushed black peppercorns

Tadka or tempering
1 tbsp butter
½ tsp cumin seeds
½ tsp mustard seeds
4–5 curry leaves
2 dried red chilies

To garnish
1 tbsp chopped mint leaves
1 tbsp chopped cilantro leaves
juice of ½ lemon (optional)

1 To prepare the stock, mix all the ingredients together in a pan. Add 1½ quarts (liters) water and cook for 10 minutes over medium heat, skimming off the scum from the surface whenever necessary. Reduce the heat to low and simmer for an hour, then strain the stock through a sieve and set aside.

2 Heat half the oil in a heavy-bottomed saucepan over medium heat. Add half of the cardamoms, cloves, cinnamon sticks, and cumin seeds along with the turmeric and sauté for a few seconds over medium heat. Add half the onions and sauté until golden brown. Add the lentils and 1⅔ cups water. Cover the saucepan, increase the heat, and boil until the lentils are soft and broken down.

3 In another saucepan, heat the rest of the oil over medium heat. Add the remaining whole spices and onions and sauté until the onions are golden brown. Stir in the ginger and garlic paste, red chili powder, and ground coriander and cook for a few seconds. If necessary, add a tablespoon or two of water to prevent the mixture from sticking to the bottom of the pan.

4 Add the mutton and sauté for 5 minutes or until the mutton turns brown. Add the stock, cover the pan, and cook for 50–55 minutes. Once the mutton is tender, add all the vegetables and the raw mango, stir for 2 minutes, and then sprinkle over garam masala.

5 Reduce the heat to low and fold in the yogurt. Cover again and simmer for another 5 minutes, or until the vegetables and raw mango are tender. Now add the cooked lentils and stir for 3 minutes. Add salt to taste.

6 For the *tadka*, or tempering, heat the butter in a separate frying pan over medium heat. Add the cumin and mustard seeds. Once they start popping, add the curry leaves and red chilies. Stir-fry for 1 minute, then pour this tempering mixture over the *dalcha* and stir.

7 Garnish with mint and cilantro and serve hot. This gravy should be slightly sour to taste. If you feel it is not sour enough, squeeze some lemon juice over the top.

No wedding meal or special dinner is considered complete without this curry. It is almost always made with mutton or lamb, although some people prefer to use chicken. The vast popularity of this dish is due to the fact that it is pretty indestructible—whichever way you cook it, it still somehow comes out tasting good. You can make it ahead and reheat it, serve it for lunch or dinner, and eat it with any kind of rice—plain boiled to chickpea pilau (p.149)—or with *naan* or roti, plus some onion raita (p.181). It is loved by people of all ages, in all seasons, and is the ultimate comfort food.

PALAK GOSHT

SPINACH AND LAMB CURRY   **PAKISTAN**

serves 4–5
spicy and fragrant

¼ cup sunflower oil
2 large onions, finely sliced
1 tsp garlic paste
2 medium tomatoes, peeled and chopped
1 tsp red chili powder
1 tsp ground turmeric
1 tsp cumin seeds
salt
1¼ lb (500 g) boned leg of lamb, cut in small pieces
1¼ lb (500 g) fresh spinach leaves or well-drained frozen spinach

To garnish
chopped green chilies
slivers of fresh ginger root

1 Heat the oil in a saucepan, add the onions, and cook until slightly browned. Add the garlic paste and tomatoes and stir for a minute. Add the chili powder, turmeric, cumin seeds, and salt to taste and stir. If necessary, add 1–2 tbsp water to prevent the mixture from sticking to the bottom of the pan and burning. Stir until the oil separates out.

2 Now add the lamb pieces together with 1½–2 cups water. Put the lid on and leave to cook over medium-low heat for 30–40 minutes. Add the spinach and continue cooking, covered, for 12–15 minutes or until the lamb is tender.

3 Remove the lid and simmer for a further 10–15 minutes or until excess liquid has evaporated and the oil separates out. Garnish with chopped green chilies and slivers of ginger, and serve.

NOTE You can make the curry in advance (it's great for freezing) and reheat it in the pan over low heat or in a microwave.

Make this curry when tomatoes are in peak season and full of flavor—Tamatar Gosht is simply pieces of lamb and lots of tomatoes cooked into a curry. Lamb (or mutton) works well with the slightly sharp taste of tomatoes; however, beef or veal shoulder or rump can be substituted for the lamb, as can chicken, quail, fish, or even squid. Serve with plum chutney (p.175) and leavened roti (p.160) or *naan*.

TAMATAR GOSHT

LAMB AND TOMATO CURRY   PAKISTAN

serves 2-3
tangy and slightly sweet

¼ cup sunflower oil
1 large onion, finely chopped
1 tsp ginger paste
½ tsp garlic paste
1¼ lb (500 g) tomatoes, peeled and chopped
salt
1 tsp red chili powder
1 tsp cumin seeds

3 black cardamom pods
5 cloves
1 bay leaf
1¼ lb (500 g) boned lamb leg or shoulder, cut into small pieces
¼ cup chopped cilantro leaves

To garnish
slivers of fresh ginger root
chopped green chilies

1 Heat the oil in a saucepan, add the onion, and fry until slightly browned. Add the ginger and garlic pastes and stir, then add the tomatoes. Add some salt, the chili powder, cumin seeds, cardamoms, cloves, and bay leaf. Stir until the oil separates out.

2 Add the lamb and fry, stirring, for 5 minutes. Pour in 1 cup water and stir well, then put the lid on the saucepan and reduce the heat to medium-low. Cook for 45–60 minutes or until the lamb is cooked and tender.

3 Remove the lid and keep cooking gently, stirring, until the oil separates out. Stir in the chopped cilantro leaves. Garnish with the ginger and green chilies, and serve.

NOTE You can make the curry in advance (it's good for freezing) and reheat it in the pan over low heat or in a microwave.

This rich and aromatic mutton stew is a traditional Muslim dish cooked during festivals and other special occasions. It is a simple dish but requires a considerable amount of time to prepare. There are various methods of cooking Nihari—this recipe uses the traditional Pakistani way to prepare this flavorful dish.

NIHARI GOSHT

SLOW-COOKED MUTTON STEW   PAKISTAN

serves 5
rich and aromatic

4 tbsp ghee
4 medium-sized onions, sliced
2¼ lb (1 kg) mutton with bones, washed, chopped into cubes
1 tsp ginger paste
½ tsp ground turmeric
1 tbsp red chili powder
4 cardamom pods
4 cloves
2 cinnamon sticks
1 tsp black peppercorns
1 tsp cumin seeds
3 tbsp yogurt, whisked until smooth
2 tbsp brown onion paste (p.166)
¼ tsp ground garam masala
¼ tsp ground fennel seeds
¼ tsp dried ground ginger
2 pinches of ground mace
2 pinches of ground nutmeg
salt
2 tbsp refined white flour

Garnish
1 tbsp finely chopped cilantro leaves
½ tsp finely chopped ginger
1 tsp chopped green chilies
¼ oz (10 g) fried onion

Stock
2¼ lb (1 kg) mutton bones
5 mutton leg pieces, each 2 in (5 cm) long, cleaned and roasted
3 cinnamon sticks
10 cardamom pods
7 cloves
1 tsp cumin seeds
1 tbsp fennel seeds
1 tsp crushed dried ginger
salt

1 To prepare the stock, take a large pot and add the mutton bones and roasted leg pieces along with 1 quart (liter) water. Boil over high heat for 5 minutes. Drain the water to remove the scum. Add another 2 quarts (liters) water along with the rest of the ingredients for the stock and boil. Reduce the heat to low and simmer for 60–90 minutes. You could add the Nihari spice potli (p.174) to enhance the flavor of the stock. Pour the stock through a sieve into a bowl and set aside.

2 Meanwhile, in a heavy-bottomed saucepan, heat the ghee over medium heat. Add the onions and sauté for 3–4 minutes or until brown. Add the mutton and cook for 3–4 minutes, stirring continuously, until light brown.

3 Stir in the ginger paste and cook for a minute. Add the turmeric, chili powder, cardamoms, cloves, cinnamon sticks, peppercorns, and cumin seeds and sauté for 2 minutes. Add 2 tbsp water and cook for a minute, stirring constantly. Reduce the heat to low, slowly fold in the yogurt, and mix well.

4 Pour the stock into the saucepan, cover, and simmer for about 1 hour. Once the mutton is three-quarters cooked, add the brown onion paste, mix well, cover, and simmer for another 40 minutes. (Check if the meat is cooked by piercing a mutton piece with a fork. If the piece starts to break but does not fall apart, it is three-quarters cooked.)

5 Uncover the saucepan, add the rest of the spices, cover, and simmer for 10 seconds. Season to taste.

6 Mix the refined white flour with a little water to make a paste. Add the paste to the gravy and mix well to acquire a slightly thick consistency.

7 Garnish with the cilantro, ginger, green chilies, and fried onion and serve with rogini *naan*.

Until the late 18th century, pork was not used much in Indian cooking. Although most of the country was Hindu and consumption of pork was not barred, a large proportion of the population was vegetarian. It was only in Anglo-Indian cooking and in the hills in the eastern part of the country that people consumed pork. This recipe originates from Darjeeling, a hill station very popular during the British Raj. The term *bhooni* refers to the dry, almost coating consistency of the spices that remain on the pork chops when the dish is finished.

PORK CHOP BHOONI

MASALA PORK CHOPS   NORTH INDIA—BENGAL

serves 4
hot and fatty

8 pork chops, about 4 oz
   (100 g) each,
   excess fat trimmed
1 tsp salt
1 tsp red chili powder
1 tbsp corn oil

Masala
1½ tbsp mild chili powder
1 tsp ground turmeric
1 tbsp ginger paste
1 tsp garlic paste
3 tomatoes, finely chopped
¼ cup corn oil

½ tsp fenugreek seeds
20 curry leaves
2 large onions, finely sliced
2 tbsp tomato ketchup
1 tsp salt
1 tsp caster sugar
1 tsp ground garam masala

To garnish
2 large potatoes, peeled and
   cut lengthwise
½ tsp salt
½ tsp ground turmeric
2 tbsp corn oil
2 tbsp chopped cilantro leaves

1 Sprinkle the pork chops with the salt and chili powder and rub in well. Heat the oil in a large, heavy pan and sear the pork chops for 2 minutes on each side or until they are colored. Remove from the pan and set aside.

2 For the masala, mix together the chili powder, turmeric, ginger and garlic pastes, and tomatoes in a bowl. Set aside.

3 Heat the ¼ cup corn oil in the pan, add the fenugreek seeds, and stir for a minute. As the seeds begin to brown, add the curry leaves and onions and sauté for 6–8 minutes or until the onions begin to turn golden brown. Add the tomato mixture to the pan and sauté for a further 3–5 minutes or until the spices are fragrant.

4 Return the seared chops to the pan, and stir in the tomato ketchup, salt, and sugar. Spoon the spice mixture over the chops to coat them evenly. Reduce the heat to low and add ¾ cup water. Simmer, covered, for 15–20 minutes or until the chops are cooked through and tender.

5 While the chops are cooking, prepare the garnish. Cook the potatoes in boiling water seasoned with the salt and turmeric for 6–8 minutes or until they are just tender but still firm. Drain. Heat the oil in a frying pan, add the potatoes, and cook until crisp and golden. Keep hot.

6 Remove the chops from the pan, transfer to a serving platter, and keep warm. Continue to cook the sauce, uncovered, for a few more minutes, until it has a thick coating consistency. Finish by stirring in the garam masala.

7 Pour the sauce over the pork chops. Arrange the crisp potatoes around the edge and sprinkle with the chopped cilantro. If you like, serve with chapatti, rice, or even some crusty bread.

Vindaloo (from the Portuguese *vindalho*) originates from Goa, where the cooking combines Portuguese influences with fiery Indian flavors. Families in Goa make vindaloo dishes for their Christmas celebrations. What makes a vindaloo dish unusual is the combination of curry spices and vinegar. This is an elaborate dish but worth the effort. If you can handle spicy food, be more generous with the chili. This is traditionally eaten with red rice, although plain rice is good, too.

PORK VINDALOO

SOUTH INDIA

serves 4
fiery hot and sour

2 lb (900 g) boned pork, cut into 2-in (5-cm) cubes
4 tbsp vegetable oil
5 garlic cloves, finely chopped
2 onions, chopped
1 tsp ground turmeric
½ tsp chili powder
½ tsp tomato paste
3 tomatoes, chopped
3 tbsp wine or cider vinegar
salt
pinch of crushed black peppercorns
1 tbsp chopped cilantro leaves

Spice paste
1 tsp cumin seeds
4 cardamom pods
4 cloves
1-in (2.5-cm) cinnamon stick
5 black peppercorns
1 green chili, chopped
1-in (2.5-cm) piece fresh ginger root, chopped
4 garlic cloves, peeled
3 tbsp lemon juice

1 To make the spice paste, grind the cumin seeds, cardamom pods, cloves, cinnamon stick, and peppercorns to a fine powder in a clean coffee grinder or spice mill. Blend the spice powder with the green chili, ginger, garlic, and lemon juice in a food processor to make a fine paste.

2 Mix the pork with the spice paste in a large bowl. Cover it with plastic wrap, then leave to marinate in a cool place for 1½ hours.

3 Heat the oil in a frying pan, add the garlic, and sauté for 1 minute. Add the onions and cook until they are golden, stirring occasionally. Add the turmeric, chili powder, tomato paste, chopped tomatoes, and vinegar and stir well.

4 Add the marinated pork and salt to taste. Cook for 10 minutes, stirring occasionally. Pour in 1 cup water and bring to a boil, then reduce the heat and simmer for 30 minutes or until the meat is cooked through and the sauce is thick.

5 Add the black pepper, then serve hot, garnished with the chopped cilantro.

The word *passanda* means a thin slice of meat, usually beef or veal, although lamb is also sometimes used. Prepared like this, a simple piece of meat is transformed into a lavish dish. The curry is ideal for any occasion and is best served with mint raita (p.180) and roti or *naan*. A less expensive cut of beef or veal can be used, as long as it is very lean and tender.

PASSANDA CURRY

SLICED BEEF CURRY   **PAKISTAN**

serves 4–5
thick and warmly spiced

1¼ lb (500 g) fillet of beef
3 tbsp sunflower oil
2 large onions, finely chopped
1 tsp garlic paste
1 tsp ginger paste
1 large tomato, peeled and
  finely chopped
5–6 tbsp chopped cilantro
  leaves

Marinade
7 oz (200 g) plain Greek-style
  yogurt
1 tsp red chili powder
½ tsp ground turmeric
1 tsp ground black pepper
1 tsp cumin seeds
1 tsp ground coriander
salt

1 Cut the beef into ¼-in (5-mm) slices. With a meat mallet, beat the slices until they are even thinner. Mix together the yogurt, spices, and salt to taste. Add the slices of beef and turn to coat with the spiced yogurt. Leave to marinate for 2–3 hours.

2 Heat the oil in a saucepan, add the onions, and cook until lightly browned. Stir in the garlic and ginger pastes, then immediately add the tomato. Stir for a few minutes. Add the marinated beef with all the spiced yogurt. Stir around for 1 minute, then put the lid on the saucepan and turn the heat to low. Cook for 15–20 minutes or until the beef is very tender.

3 Remove the lid and stir for a few more minutes or until the oil separates out. Stir in ¼ cup of the chopped cilantro. Garnish with the remaining chopped cilantro and serve.

NOTE You can make this curry in advance (it's good for freezing) and reheat it in the pan over low heat or in a microwave.

This is a fascinating recipe that comes from the kitchens of a very wealthy *maharani* in central India. I like it because it's very easy to remember and very simple to make. It strangely resembles a pound cake recipe from the medieval era, where you put in equal quantities of everything, mix it up, and pop it in the oven. In this case, just mix together all the ingredients and cover the pan. Cook either in the oven or on the stovetop over very low heat. The recipe here uses goat, but feel free to replace it with lamb or mutton—both work just as well.

REZALA

BHOPAL-STYLE GOAT CURRY   NORTH INDIA—LUCKNOW & AWADH

serves 4
hot, spicy, and rich

2¼ lb (1 kg) boned leg of goat, cut into 1-in (2.5-cm) cubes
¾ cup corn oil or ghee
7 oz (200 g) green chilies, slit lengthwise and seeded
7 oz (200 g) crisp-fried onions, crushed coarsely
2 tbsp pineapple, blended to a paste
7 oz (200 g) plain Greek-style yogurt
2 tbsp finely chopped fresh ginger root
1 tbsp garlic paste
3 tbsp roasted chickpea flour
1 tbsp salt

1 tsp whole allspice
2 tsp royal cumin or black cumin seeds
2 tsp red chili powder
2 tsp ground cumin
2 tsp ground garam masala
Layered paratha dough (p.154), or a flour and water dough, to seal

To finish
⅓ cup heavy cream
2 oz (50 g) fried cashew nuts, pounded or blended to a paste
½ cup chopped cilantro leaves
2 tbsp chopped mint leaves

1 If cooking in the oven, preheat it to 350°F (180°C).

2 Mix the meat with all the other ingredients except the paratha dough, and set aside to marinate for 10–15 minutes.

3 Transfer the marinated meat to an ovenproof earthenware casserole dish or ovenproof pan with a tight-fitting lid. Seal the lid using paratha dough. If need be, place a weight on the lid to prevent steam from escaping during cooking.

4 Put the casserole in the oven or the pot over low heat. Cook for 2 hours or until the meat is tender. If cooking in the oven, reduce the heat to 250°F (110°C) after 25–30 minutes.

5 Stir the sauce, then finish by adding the cream and cashew nut paste. Bring back to a boil. Taste and adjust the seasoning, if required. Sprinkle with the chopped cilantro and mint and serve.

This is an extremely popular Pakistani curry. It is a simple and quick yet tasty, wholesome dish that can be served as part of a regular meal and also when entertaining.

KEEMA ALOO

GROUND MEAT AND POTATO CURRY   PAKISTAN

serves 5
aromatic and spiced

7 oz (200 g) ghee
7 green cardamom pods
7 cloves
3 cinnamon sticks, each
   2 in (5 cm) long
3 bay leaves
1 tsp cumin seeds
3 onions, finely chopped
1 tbsp garlic paste
2¼ lb (1 kg) ground goat or
   lamb, leg piece
10 oz (300 g) tomatoes,
   finely chopped

6 green chilies, slit lengthwise
9 oz (250 g) plain yogurt
10 oz (300 g) large potatoes,
   peeled and cut into 1-in
   (2.5-cm) cubes
1 tbsp Kashmiri chili powder
1 tbsp ground coriander
½ tsp ground turmeric
1 tbsp ground garam masala
1 tsp black peppercorns
salt
1 tbsp, finely chopped cilantro
   leaves, to garnish

1 To make the masala, heat the ghee in a heavy-bottomed saucepan over medium heat. Add the cardamoms, cloves, cinnamon sticks, and bay leaves and sauté for 2–3 minutes. Add the cumin seeds and fry until brown.

2 Stir in the onions and sauté for 5 minutes or until golden brown. Mix in the garlic paste and fry until brown.

3 Now add the meat and cook for 10 minutes, stirring frequently. Mix in the tomatoes, half of the green chilies, and the yogurt and sauté for another 8–10 minutes.

4 Add the potatoes along with the chili powder, ground coriander, turmeric, garam masala, and peppercorns. Season and cook for 7–8 minutes, stirring frequently. Cover the pan, reduce the heat to low, and simmer until the potatoes and meat are tender and cooked.

5 Remove the whole spices and transfer to a serving dish. Garnish with the cilantro and the remaining green chilies and serve hot with *rogini naan* or *roti*.

This is the type of dish that would have been cooked on a *shikaar*, or hunting expedition, when the Rajput princes went out hunting with their entourage. It would originally have been made with hare but works just as well with rabbit.

ACHARI KHARGOSH

RABBIT LEG COOKED IN PICKLING SPICES   **NORTH INDIA—RAJASTHAN**

serves 4
spicy, tangy, and sour

4–6 rabbit legs, about 2 lb (900 g) in total
1 tsp salt
1 tsp ground turmeric

Sauce
3½ tbsp mustard oil
⅓ cup ghee
4 dried red chilies
1 tbsp mixed pickling spices (p.18)
8 garlic cloves, finely chopped
2 onions, about 6 oz (150 g) in total, finely chopped
1 tsp salt
½ tsp ground turmeric
1-in (2.5-cm) piece fresh ginger root, cut into julienne strips
2 tbsp palm sugar or molasses
10 oz (300 g) plain full-fat yogurt
2 tsp chickpea flour
juice of 1 lemon
1 tbsp finely chopped cilantro leaves

1 Place the rabbit legs in a pan and add the salt and turmeric. Pour in 1½ quarts (liters) water and bring to a boil over medium heat. Reduce the heat to low, cover with a lid, and simmer for 45 minutes or until tender. Remove the rabbit legs from the liquid and drain; reserve the cooking liquid.

2 In another heavy-bottomed pan, heat the mustard oil to smoking point over medium heat. Add the ghee and, as it melts, add the whole red chilies and allow them to crackle for a few seconds. Next, add the pickling spices and, as they begin to crackle and change color, add the garlic. Sauté the garlic for a minute or so until golden brown, then add the onions. Sauté for 10 minutes or until the onions are soft and translucent but not brown.

3 Stir in the salt and turmeric and add the cooked rabbit legs. Add the ginger and palm sugar and stir for a few minutes, until the legs start to acquire a light brown color. Now stir in the reserved cooking liquid and let it simmer for 5 minutes.

4 In a bowl, whisk the yogurt with the chickpea flour until well combined. Increase the heat and bring the liquid in the pan back to a boil. Slowly add the yogurt mixture, stirring constantly to prevent it from separating. When all the yogurt has been incorporated, continue simmering for 2–3 minutes. It's fine if the oil starts to separate out at the sides of the pan.

5 Adjust the seasoning and, just before serving, stir in the lemon juice and cilantro. Serve with either rice or bread.

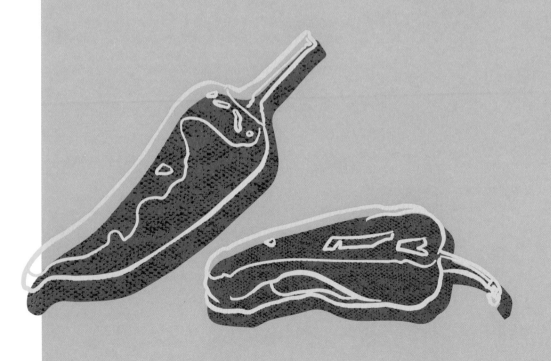

RICE AND BREAD

This is one of the simplest pilau rice preparations that you will ever come across. Traditionally in Lucknow and central states, pilaus were of many varieties and often used several ingredients together. The basic difference between boiled rice and pilau rice is not the use of spices but the method of cooking. Boiled rice may be cooked with spices, but the cooking liquid is drained away at the end, similar to when cooking pasta. For pilau rice, it is important to use just the right quantity of water, because it should all be absorbed when the rice is done. Rice has more flavor and nutrients when cooked by the pilau method.

MUTTER PULAO

GREEN PEA PILAU   **NORTH INDIA—LUCKNOW & AWADH**

serves 4
deliciously perfumed

14 oz (400 g) basmati rice
⅓ cup ghee
1 tsp cumin seeds
½ tsp cloves
1 cinnamon leaf or bay leaf

4 green cardamom pods
1 cinnamon stick
2 red onions, finely sliced
4 oz (100 g) frozen peas, thawed
1 tbsp salt
2 tsp shredded mint leaves
2 tsp chopped cilantro leaves

1 Wash the rice in cold running water, then soak in enough cold water to cover for 20–25 minutes. Soaking the rice reduces the cooking time and prevents the grains from breaking while cooking.

2 Heat the ghee in a heavy-bottomed Dutch oven over medium heat and add the whole spices. When they crackle, add the sliced onions and sauté until they are golden brown. Add the peas and sauté for 2–3 minutes. Pour in 3½ cups water. Add the salt, cover, and bring to a boil.

3 Drain the soaked rice and add to the casserole pot. Cover again and bring back to a boil. Cook, covered, for 8–10 minutes over medium-high heat. From time to time, remove the lid and gently stir the rice, keeping in mind that too much handling can break the rice grains.

4 When the water is nearly all absorbed and you can see small holes on the surface of the rice, sprinkle the mint and the cilantro over it. Cover the casserole dish tightly and reduce the heat to low. Cook for a further 10 minutes. Alternatively, finish cooking the rice in a preheated 250°F (130°C) oven for 10 minutes.

NOTE To make the pilau in a microwave, follow the recipe up to the stage of adding the peas. Then add the salt and the soaked rice and mix lightly for a couple of minutes, until the grains of rice are coated with oil. Transfer to a microwave container. Pour the measured quantity of water over the rice, cover with plastic wrap, and pierce it to make a few holes. Place in the microwave and cook for 18–20 minutes. Allow the rice to rest for 5 minutes, then transfer to a serving dish.

This is a basic dish of boiled basmati rice enriched with the addition of ghee. The nuttiness of ghee combined with the texture of sea salt is simple cooking at its very best. Normally you will find cooking times on the packaging of basmati rice, so follow these if they are given.

GHEE BHAAT

GHEE RICE   **NORTH INDIA—BENGAL**

serves 8–10

1 lb 2 oz (500 g) basmati rice
3 tbsp ghee
1 tbsp flaked sea salt

1 Wash the rice in cold running water, then leave to soak in enough cold water to cover for 20–25 minutes. Soaking the rice reduces the cooking time and prevents the grains from breaking while cooking.

2 Meanwhile, bring 2 quarts (liters) water to a boil in a large saucepan. When the water is boiling, add the drained rice. Bring back to a boil, then cook, uncovered, over medium-high heat for 10–14 minutes or until the rice is just cooked. It should not be al dente, like pasta, but neither should it be overcooked so that it disintegrates.

3 Drain the rice in a colander and, while the rice is still hot, add the ghee and sea salt and mix well. Serve immediately. If the rice gets cold, you can reheat it in the microwave for 1–2 minutes.

In this typical dish of the Brahmin community of southern India, mixed lentils are cooked with basmati rice to introduce a nutty, aromatic flavor. It's a rich dish and can be eaten as complete meal.

BISSI BELA BHATH

MIXED VEGETABLE RICE   **SOUTH INDIA**

serves 4
nutty, aromatic, and rich

6 oz (150 g) split yellow lentils (*toor dal*)
2 tbsp vegetable oil
2½ oz (75 g) freshly grated coconut
7 dried red chilies
2 tsp coriander seeds
1 tsp split gram lentils (*chana dal*)
1 tsp split black lentils (*urad dal*)
1 tsp ground turmeric

½ tsp fenugreek seeds
pinch of asafetida
1 lb 2 oz (500 g) basmati rice
salt
½ cup tamarind water, made with 1¾ oz (50 g) pulp and ½ cup water (p.172)

For tempering
2 tbsp vegetable oil
1 tsp mustard seeds
10 curry leaves
1 tbsp chopped raw cashew nuts

1 Bring 2 cups water to a boil in a large saucepan. Add the yellow lentils and simmer until tender. Drain and set aside.

2 Heat the oil in a frying pan and add the coconut, red chilies, coriander seeds, split gram and black lentils, turmeric, fenugreek seeds, and asafetida. Fry until fragrant. Allow to cool, then grind to a fine powder in a clean coffee grinder or spice mill.

3 Clean the rice in cold running water, then place it in a large saucepan. Add 1 quart (liter) water and a little salt. Bring to a boil, then simmer for about 20 minutes.

4 Add the yellow lentils, tamarind water, and spiced coconut powder. Cook for a further 5 minutes. Add just a little more water if the mixture becomes very dry too quickly.

5 Meanwhile, for the tempering, heat the oil in a frying pan and add the mustard seeds. As they begin to pop, add the curry leaves and cashew nuts and cook, stirring, until the nuts turn golden brown. Pour the mixture over the cooked rice, mix together, and serve hot.

Rice preparations are very common in Tamil Nadu and Karnataka. The addition of nuts and lentils and careful spicing make this rice dish very savory and colorful. It goes well with all kinds of curries, be they meat, fish, poultry, or vegetable.

PULI CHORU

TAMARIND RICE   **SOUTH INDIA**

serves 4
fragrant, rich, and savory

1¾ oz (50 g) tamarind pulp
1¼ cups long-grain or basmati rice
salt
2 tbsp vegetable oil
1 tsp mustard seeds
1 onion, finely chopped
¾ oz (20 g) raw peanuts

1 tbsp split gram lentils (*chana dal*) or split yellow lentils (*toor dal*)
10 curry leaves
3 dried red chilies
1 tsp fenugreek seeds
1 tsp asafetida
1 tsp chili powder
1 tsp ground coriander
1 tsp ground turmeric
1 tbsp chopped cilantro leaves

1 Bring ½ cup water to a boil in a small saucepan. Add the tamarind pulp and simmer for 10 minutes, stirring occasionally. Strain the thick tamarind water into a bowl and set aside.

2 In a large saucepan, bring 2 cups of water to a boil. Add the rice and a little salt to taste. Allow to cook for 20–25 minutes or until the rice is tender. Drain and keep warm.

3 Rinse the saucepan, then heat it and pour in the oil. When the oil is hot, add the mustard seeds. As they begin to pop, add the onion, peanuts, lentils, curry leaves, dried chilies, and fenugreek seeds. Cook, stirring frequently, until the onions are soft.

4 Add the asafetida, chili powder, ground coriander, turmeric, and some salt. Cook over medium heat, stirring, for 2–3 minutes. Pour in the tamarind water. Mix well and cook for 15 minutes.

5 Add the rice and stir to combine, then transfer to a bowl. Garnish with the chopped cilantro.

This is a great combination of protein and carbohydrates and makes a complete meal if served with a salad and yogurt. It can be made spicy or mild, according to your taste. A rice dish like this is a good way to introduce people—including children—to the wonderful world of curries. It can be packed into lunchboxes to take to school or work and is perfect eaten outdoors on a warm summer evening.

CHANA PULAO

CHICKPEA PILAU   **PAKISTAN**

serves 5
aromatic and hearty

1¼ lb (500 g) basmati rice
½ cup sunflower oil
4 oz (115 g) thinly sliced onion
1 tsp fresh ginger root, cut in
   slivers
3 cinnamon sticks
1 tsp black peppercorns
1 tsp cumin seeds

3 black cardamom pods
salt
4 oz (115 g) dried chickpeas,
   soaked overnight and cooked
   until tender, or 14 oz (400 g)
   canned chickpeas, drained

Fried brown onions
2 tbsp sunflower oil
1 large onion, thinly sliced

1 Thoroughly wash the rice in cold running water, then leave to soak in a bowl with enough water to cover for at least 1 hour. Drain.

2 Heat the oil in a saucepan, add the onion, and fry until golden brown. Add the ginger, all the spices, and salt to taste and stir for about 1 minute. Add 3 cups water and bring to a boil. Add the soaked rice and cooked or canned chickpeas. Cover the saucepan, reduce the heat, and simmer for about 15 minutes or until the rice is about 90 percent cooked.

3 Dampen a clean, thick dishcloth with water. Remove the lid from the saucepan. Cover with the cloth, then put the lid back on tightly and set the pan over very low heat. (You can place the saucepan in a heavy frying pan to further reduce the heat.) Cook like this for 25–30 minutes.

4 Meanwhile, heat the oil in a large saucepan, add the onion, and cook until dark golden brown and crisp. Remove the onion with a slotted spoon and drain on paper towels.

5 Garnish the pilau with the fried brown onions and serve.

If you want a rice dish that is more than a rice dish—one that is versatile, colorful, and can show your masterly skills—then this is the one to make. It is appropriate with any curry or condiment, is great for picnics and barbecues, can be eaten hot or cold, and children love it. You can use any vegetables that are in season.

SUBZI BIRYANI

VEGETABLE BIRYANI   **PAKISTAN**

serves 4–5
colorful and aromatic

1¼ lb (500 g) basmati rice
½ cup sunflower oil
2 large onions, sliced
1 tsp ginger paste
1 tsp garlic paste
8 oz (225 g) peeled and
  finely chopped tomatoes
1 tsp red chili powder
1 tsp ground turmeric
1 tsp ground coriander
2 cinnamon sticks
4 black cardamom pods
1 tsp cumin seeds

1 tsp black peppercorns
1 tsp cloves
4 star anise
2 bay leaves
salt
9 oz (250 g) plain Greek-style
  yogurt
9 oz (250 g) potatoes, peeled
  and diced
6 oz (150 g) shelled fresh or
  frozen peas
6 oz (150 g) carrots, peeled
  and diced
4 tbsp finely chopped cilantro
  leaves
fried brown onions to garnish
  (p.149)

1 Thoroughly wash the rice in cold running water, then leave to soak in enough water to cover for at least 1 hour. Drain the rice and cook in plenty of boiling salted water until it is 90 percent cooked. Drain the rice and set aside.

2 Heat the oil in a saucepan, add the onions, and fry until golden brown. Add the ginger and garlic pastes and cook for 1 minute, then stir in the tomatoes, all the spices, the bay leaves, some salt, and the yogurt. Cook for about 10 minutes or until the oil separates out.

3 Add the potatoes, fresh peas, and carrots with ½ cup water and cook for 5–8 minutes or until the vegetables are tender. (If using frozen, add peas when the potatoes and carrots are almost done.) Remove from the heat.

4 Spread half the cooked rice over the bottom of a large saucepan. Put the cooked vegetables on this layer of rice and sprinkle with the chopped cilantro. Cover with the remaining rice.

5 Dampen a clean, thick dishcloth with water and cover the saucepan. Put the lid tightly on the cloth and set the saucepan on very low heat. (You can place the saucepan in a heavy frying pan to further reduce the heat.) Cook like this for about 30 minutes.

6 Mix the rice gently with the vegetables, then spoon into a large, flat dish. Garnish with fried brown onions and serve.

This rustic, spiced bread uses two different flours along with spices and seasoning, which gives it a unique flavor. It was a favorite for travelers, who would carry some of this bread to have with small quantities of very spicy garlic chutney for a light meal during their journey. Chickpea flour increases water retention in the body, which is particularly useful when traveling in the desert. The bread can be served either as an accompaniment to any Rajasthani recipe in this book or as a snack with a chutney or pickle of your choice.

MISSI ROTI

CHICKPEA BREAD   **NORTH INDIA—RAJASTHAN**

makes 8

2½ cups chickpea flour
1⅔ cups all-purpose flour
4 tsp salt
1 tsp finely chopped fresh ginger root
2 green chilies, seeded and finely chopped
1 tbsp finely chopped cilantro leaves
1 tsp carom seeds
½ tsp red chili powder
½ tsp ground turmeric
2 tbsp vegetable oil
1 red onion, finely chopped
1 green onion, finely chopped
3 tbsp melted ghee for brushing and basting

1 Mix together the chickpea flour and all-purpose flour in a large bowl. Transfer 3–4 tbsp of the flour mix to a small bowl and set aside to use later if needed. Add the salt, ginger, green chilies, chopped cilantro, carom seeds, red chili powder, and turmeric to the large bowl and mix well to combine with the flours.

2 Add the oil and ¾ cup water and knead to obtain a stiff dough. If the dough feels slightly soft, add some of the reserved flour. Gather the dough into a mound; cover with a clean, damp dishcloth; and set aside for 15–20 minutes.

3 Divide the dough into 8 pieces and shape into balls. Top each of the balls with chopped red onion and green onion, then roll out using a rolling pin into a round 6–8 in (15–20 cm) in diameter.

4 Place a large frying pan over low to medium heat. When hot, cook the breads on the dry pan, one at a time, for 3–4 minutes on each side or until they start to dry out and color.

5 When both sides are done, brush with some melted ghee and turn the bread over, then brush the other side with melted ghee. Serve the breads hot.

Cooks prepare these triangular breads in thousands of households across northern India almost every morning to eat for breakfast, lunch, and dinner. You can add different spices, chilies, pastes, and so on to create your own unique paratha.

TAWA PARATHA

LAYERED PARATHA

NORTH INDIA—LUCKNOW & AWADH

makes 8

4 cups chapatti flour
2 tsp salt
1 tbsp vegetable oil
½ cup chapatti flour to dust
3 tbsp melted ghee or
  vegetable oil
1 tbsp carom seeds or black
  onion seeds (optional)

1 Mix the chapatti flour with the salt, oil, and 1 cup plus 2 tbsp water in a large bowl to make a smooth dough.

2 Cover with a damp cloth or plastic wrap and leave to rest for 15 minutes.

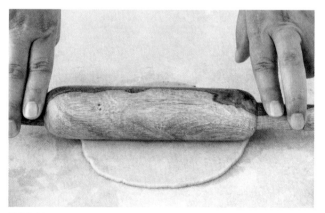

3 Divide the dough into 8 equal portions and shape each into a smooth ball. Take one ball at a time and flatten it. Dust with some of the extra flour and, using a rolling pin, roll it out into a disk 2½–3 in (6–8 cm) in diameter.

4 Spread a little ghee on the surface of the disk, sprinkle with some seeds (if using), and dust with a little flour. Fold the disk in half to form a half-moon.

5 Repeat the same process of ghee, seeds, and flour on the surface of the half-moon, then fold into a triangle. Now flatten the triangle carefully using the rolling pin until it is about ⅛ in (3 mm) thick.

6 Heat a dry tawa, griddle, or frying pan and fry each bread for a couple of minutes, until the surface is dry and it starts to get specks of brown. Turn it over and cook for a further 2 minutes.

7 While the second side is cooking, brush the first side lightly with ghee. Turn the bread over again and brush the other side with ghee. You should see the steam opening up the layers as the bread cooks.

8 Remove from the heat once both sides are golden and crisp. Serve the breads hot from the pan.

Poories, or *luchis* as they are called in Bengal, are an excellent accompaniment to dry curries, as well as being very popular with children as a snack or even as picnic bread. In Bengal, they sometimes use a tad more oil or ghee when making their dough, which produces a shorter and crisper bread, and they also use refined white flour more than whole-wheat flour, which is the norm in the rest of India. In addition, the Bengalis like to add some onion and carom seeds, which makes the bread dramatic in appearance, more flavorful, and easier to digest.

POORIES

DEEP-FRIED PUFFED BREADS   **NORTH INDIA—BENGAL**

makes 20

1 lb 2 oz (500 g) chapatti flour,
  all-purpose flour,
  or a mixture of the two (half
  of each)
2 tsp salt

1 tsp sugar
1 tsp carom seeds
1 tsp black onion seeds
1 tbsp ghee or oil
vegetable oil for deep-frying
2 tbsp vegetable oil for rolling

1 Mix together the flour, salt, sugar, and seeds in a bowl. Rub in the ghee with your fingers until it is thoroughly blended with the flour.

2 Make a well in the center of the flour and pour in 1 cup water little by little, mixing to make a stiff dough. Work the dough well with your hands.

3 Cover with a damp cloth and set aside for 15 minutes.

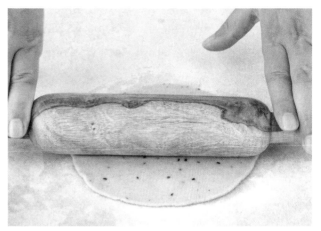

4 Divide the dough into 20 pieces and cover once more with the damp cloth. Work with one piece at a time, keeping the rest covered.

5 While oil is heating in your deep fryer or wok to about 350°F (180°C), roll each piece of dough into a smooth ball. Apply a little oil to each dough ball, then, using a rolling pin, roll out into a disk about 4 in (10 cm) in diameter.

6 Deep-fry the breads in the hot oil for 1–2 minutes or until they have puffed up and are crisp and golden on both sides.

7 Drain on paper towel and serve hot.

This humble bread from Delhi and Punjab is probably one of the best gifts from the *tandoor* to humankind. It is widely available and popular the world over and makes an excellent accompaniment for any curry. *Naan* is traditionally cooked in a charcoal-fired clay oven but will work as well in a regular oven or under the broiler. Use your imagination, and you could soon be making *naan* sandwiches and wraps or even using it as a base for canapés.

NAAN

NAAN BREAD   **NORTH INDIA—DELHI & PUNJAB**

makes 16

2 heaping tbsp caster sugar
2 eggs
1⅔ cups whole milk
6 cups all-purpose flour
1½ tsp baking powder
1 tbsp salt
3½ tbsp vegetable oil

1 Preheat the oven to 425°F (220°C). Place two nonstick baking sheets in the oven to heat up.

2 Whisk the sugar and eggs with the milk in a small mixing bowl, stirring until the sugar has dissolved. Put the flour in a large mixing bowl and mix in the baking powder and salt. Gradually pour the milk mixture into the flour, mixing with your hand, and knead lightly, just enough to make a soft dough. Take care not to knead too much or the dough will become too stretchy. Cover the bowl with a damp cloth and leave to rest for 15 minutes.

3 Add the oil and mix lightly to incorporate it into the dough. Divide the dough into 16 small pieces. Roll out each piece into a round about 4 in (10 cm) in diameter. To form into the traditional "teardrop" shape, lay a round over one palm and gently pull one edge down until it stretches a bit. Place the breads on the hot trays and bake for 4-5 minutes.

4 Serve warm. (If not serving immediately, reheat in a 350°F [180°C] oven for 1-2 minutes.)

Unlike in northern India, where wheat flour is used, breads in the south of the country are made with rice flour. This is a very light bread, spiced for a delightful change. Unlike many other breads, it can be made very quickly.

AKKI ROTTI

SAVORY RICE BREADS   **SOUTH INDIA**

serves 4

2 cups rice flour

1¾ oz (50 g) freshly grated coconut or desiccated coconut

2 tbsp chopped cilantro leaves

10 curry leaves, chopped

2 green chilies, chopped

2½ oz (75 g) shallots, finely sliced

10 cashew nuts, roasted and ground

salt

vegetable oil for frying

1 Put all the ingredients in a large bowl and mix well. Make a well in the center and gradually stir in about 2 cups of water to make soft dough. With floured hands, knead the dough to mix and shape it into small balls.

2 Roll out the balls on a surface dusted with rice flour to make disks as thin as possible. Leave to rest for 10 minutes.

3 Heat a large frying pan and coat the bottom with oil. Place one disk of dough in the pan and cook for 2–3 minutes or until golden brown. Turn over and brown the other side. Remove from the pan and keep hot while you cook the remaining breads. Serve hot.

A *roti* with ghee or butter spread over it is a match made in heaven.
Serve these slightly puffy breads hot, straight from the oven.

KHAMIRI ROTI

LEAVENED ROTI   **PAKISTAN**

makes 5-6

1 tsp dry yeast
¼ tsp sugar
1¼ lb (500 g) white or
  whole-wheat bread flour
1 tsp salt

1 Dissolve the yeast and sugar in 2 tbsp warm water, then leave for 15 minutes to become frothy.

2 Sift the flour and salt into a large mixing bowl. Add the yeast mixture and more water (about 1 cup) to make a dough. Knead for 8-10 minutes or until pliable.

3 Divide the dough into equal portions and shape each into a ball. Leave in a warm place for 30 minutes. The dough will rise slightly.

4 Preheat the oven to 350°F (180°C).

5 With a rolling pin, roll out each ball of dough to a 9-in (23-cm) disk. Place on a nonstick baking sheet and bake for 3-5 minutes or until lightly browned and a bit puffy. Serve immediately.

The crisp, crackling texture and taste of a fried *roti* goes well with just about every curry ever created. They are best freshly fried, but they can be frozen or refrigerated, then reheated in the oven (wrapped in foil), in the microwave, or in a frying pan.

PRATHA

FRIED ROTI   **PAKISTAN**

makes 4–5

2 cups white bread flour
2 cups whole-wheat flour
1¼ tsp salt
2½ tsp sunflower oil
1 cup sunflower oil for frying

1 Sift the flours and salt into a large mixing bowl. Add 1½ cups water and the 2½ tsp oil, and knead to make a pliable dough. Leave to rest for 30 minutes.

2 Divide the dough into equal portions and shape into balls. Roll out into 8-in (20-cm) diameter disks. Heat the oil for frying in a large frying pan. Fry the breads over medium heat for about 2 minutes on each side or until golden brown. Drain on paper towels and serve hot.

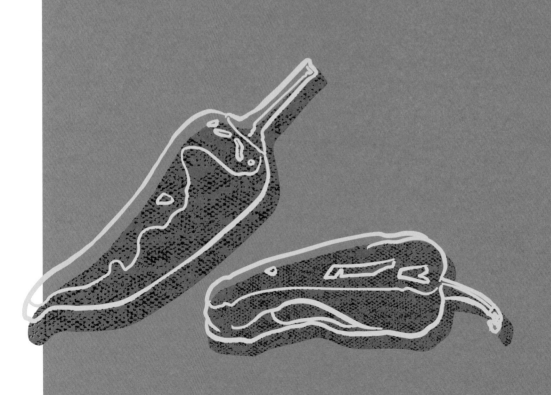

PREPPED INGREDIENTS, SAUCES, AND CHUTNEYS

The process of "clarifying" butter to produce ghee, or pure butter fat, makes it an excellent cooking medium able to withstand high temperatures and constant reheating. It also prevents it from going rancid, an important consideration in a hot country such as India. Ghee has a unique rich, nutty taste.

GHEE CLARIFIED BUTTER

Yields about ¾ cup

2 sticks (1 cup) unsalted butter

1 Place the butter in a heavy saucepan over low heat.

2 Melt the butter and bring it to a low boil.

3 Simmer the melted butter for 20–30 minutes until all the water has evaporated.

4 Skim the froth that appears on the surface and discard.

5 Continue to boil until the butter separates into cooked milk solids, which settle at the bottom of the pan, and a clear, golden ghee forms at the top.

6 Carefully strain the ghee into a bowl. Discard the solids, and leave the liquid ghee to cool.

7 Once cool, the ghee will solidify, but it will have a creamy consistency, somewhat like soft tub margarine. If refrigerated, it will become hard. Ghee can be stored for several years if kept in a tin or glass container in a cool, dark place, free from any moisture or contact with water.

This fried onion paste is used as a base in many Indian curries. It enhances the taste and adds thickness and color to the gravy. You could prepare and store this paste in the refrigerator for up to 1 week.

BROWN ONION PASTE

makes 9 oz (250 g)

1 lb 2 oz (500 g) large onions
1 cup vegetable oil
16 fl oz (500 ml) yogurt

1 Peel and wash the onions and pat dry with paper towel. Using a sharp knife, finely slice the onions.

2 Heat the oil in a heavy-bottomed pan over medium heat. Add the sliced onions and fry until golden brown. Remove the pan from the heat. Take the onions out with a slotted spoon and set aside on a plate to cool.

3 Once cooled, put the onions along with the yogurt in a blender and blend for 2–3 minutes to make a smooth paste.

4 Do not touch the paste with your fingers, as it might get spoiled. Instead, use a spatula to remove the paste. Either use immediately or transfer to an airtight container and store in the fridge for up to 1 week.

"Panch Phoran" literally translates to "five spices" and is a staple spice combination used mostly in potato and vegetable curries. The combination adds color and a distinct taste to dishes and is one of the simplest spice packages used in recipes. These spices are usually added while cooking and are either gently tossed or shallow fried (like *tadka*), giving the recipe a distinct aroma and taste.

PANCH PHORAN MASALA

serves 5

½ tsp cumin seeds
½ tsp fennel seeds
½ tsp nigella seeds
½ tsp fenugreek seeds
½ tsp mustard seeds

1 Measure out the spices and place them in separate bowls. Use whole spices for this masala mix and make sure all the spices are of the same quantity.

2 Mix together the five spices in a bowl. This panch phoran masala is used in a variety of Indian curries. You could grind, dry roast, or fry the spices, depending on the recipe you are preparing.

This aromatic blend of spices may be used whole or ground to a fine powder, depending on the dish. Whole garam masala is often added at the beginning or early in the cooking, whereas ground mixes are used to finish a dish. The basic mixture usually includes coriander seeds, cumin seeds, cardamom, cinnamon, cloves, mace, peppercorns, and cinnamon leaf in varying proportions and with other spices added according to the individual cook's preferences and the dish being prepared.

GARAM MASALA HOT SPICE MIX

Makes about 5 oz (150 g)

3 tbsp coriander seeds
3 tbsp cumin seeds
20 green cardamom pods
10 cinnamon sticks, 1 in (2.5 cm) long
2 tbsp cloves

10 blades mace
10 black cardamom pods
½ nutmeg
1 tbsp black peppercorns
4 cinnamon leaves or bay leaves
1 tbsp dried rose petals
1 tbsp fennel seeds

1 Heat a dry frying pan and add all the spices. Stir them and shake the pan as they start to crackle. When they smell roasted and aromatic, remove the pan from the heat and pour the spices onto a plate. Allow to cool.

2 To grind the spices, use a mortar and pestle or a spice mill (or a clean coffee grinder).

This paste is used in various South Indian curries and gravies. Though the paste is on the spicier side, the tamarind gives it a refreshing tanginess. Depending on the recipe you are preparing, you could also add yogurt, tomato paste, or grated coconut to this paste.

DAKSHIN CURRY PASTE

makes 1 lb 10 oz (750 g)

1 tsp mustard seeds
2 tbsp cumin seeds
2 tbsp black peppercorn
3½ oz (100 g) dried red chilies
1¾ oz (50 g) coriander seeds
scant 1 oz (25 g) tamarind
14 oz (400 g) sambar onions, peeled

1 cup vegetable oil
4 sprigs of curry leaves
3 tbsp ginger and garlic paste
1 tsp ground turmeric
salt
2 tbsp chopped cilantro leaves

1 Heat a small, heavy-bottomed frying pan or griddle over medium heat. Add the whole spices and roast for about 1 minute, stirring constantly. As soon as they start to release their flavor—the smoky smell of the spices will indicate this—remove from the heat and transfer to a plate. Set aside.

2 Meanwhile, soak the tamarind in 1 cup water for 15 minutes or until the pulp has softened. Strain the softened tamarind through a sieve into a bowl and set aside (p.172). Using a blender, grind the onions into a fine paste. Transfer the roasted spice mix to a mortar and grind to a fine powder using the pestle (p.173). Alternatively, use a blender or a small food processor.

3 Heat the oil in a frying pan, add the curry leaves and ginger and garlic paste, and sauté for 30 seconds. Now add the onion paste and sauté until the onions turn light brown.

4 Add the turmeric and sauté for 20 seconds. Mix in the tamarind water and cook for 2 minutes over low heat.

5 Add the dry spice mix and sauté for 30 seconds, stirring frequently.

6 Season to taste, sprinkle over the cilantro, and stir. Remove from the heat, cool, and store or use immediately.

This paste can be used in various chicken and vegetable curries. Curry leaves mixed with dried chilies and other spices give it a hot, lemony flavor. Mix a small quantity of the paste in a curry for a sharp but palatable taste.

MADRAS FIERY CURRY PASTE

makes 14 oz (400 g)

⅔ cup vegetable oil
1 tsp mustard seeds
5 sprigs of curry leaves
2 tsp sugar
1 tsp salt

Spice paste
6 garlic pods, peeled
¾ oz (20 g) ginger
10 dried red chilies
1 tbsp cumin seeds
1 tbsp coriander seeds
1 cup wine or malt vinegar

Dry mix
1 tsp garam masala powder
1 tbsp paprika
½ tsp ground turmeric

1 Put all the ingredients for the spice paste in a blender and grind to make a paste. Mix together the ingredients for the dry mix, add it to the spice paste, and blend.

2 Heat the oil in a frying pan. Add the mustard seeds and cook over medium heat until they crackle.

3 Add the curry leaves and sauté for 5 seconds or until the leaves begin to release their aroma.

4 Add the spice paste and cook for 10 minutes over medium heat.

5 Reduce the heat and simmer for 5 minutes or until the masala settles to the base.

6 Add sugar and salt and check the seasoning. Set aside to cool, then transfer the paste to an airtight container and store for up to 1 month.

As a general guide, use a walnut-sized piece or about 1 oz (30 g) of pulp and ½ cup water. To make thick tamarind water, use twice as much pulp.

TAMARIND WATER

1 Break a piece of tamarind pulp from the block, put it in a bowl, and cover with hot water.

2 Leave to soak for 10–15 minutes or until the pulp has softened, then squeeze and mash the pulp with your fingers to loosen and separate the fibers and seeds.

3 Strain the thick brown water through a sieve into a bowl; discard the solids. Tamarind water can be stored in the refrigerator for 2 weeks.

Dry-roasting whole spices makes them more aromatic and brings out their flavor. It also dries them and makes them easier to grind to a powder.

ROASTING AND GRINDING SPICES

1 Heat a small, heavy-bottomed frying pan or griddle over medium heat. Add the whole spices and roast for about 1 minute, stirring constantly or shaking the pan to prevent the spices from scorching.

2 As soon as they start to darken and you catch the spicy aroma, remove from the heat and pour the spices onto a plate. Cool.

3 Transfer the spices to a mortar and grind to a fine powder using the pestle. Alternatively, use a spice mill or clean electric coffee grinder.

4 For a very fine result, pass the powder through a sieve to remove any remaining bits of husks and seed.

Whole spices add depth to any recipe with their woody, wholesome flavors. This bouquet garni is a mixture of aromatic Asian spices and is used in slow-cooked mutton recipes and mutton stock in the India and Pakistan region.

NIHARI SPICE POTLI

2 onions, roughly chopped
¾ oz (20 g) ginger
scant 1 oz (25 g) cilantro leaves
scant 1 oz (25 g) mint leaves
¼ oz (10 g) vetiver roots
5 garlic cloves
6 black cardamom pods
6 cloves
2 cinnamon sticks

2 bay leaves
1 tsp black peppercorns
1 tsp cumin seeds
pinch of grated nutmeg
2 blades mace
2 star anise
¼ oz (10 g) dried rose petals
1 tsp caraway seeds

1 Roughly chop the onions, ginger, cilantro, mint, and vetiver roots. Roughly crush the garlic cloves. Place all the ingredients on a plate and mix together.

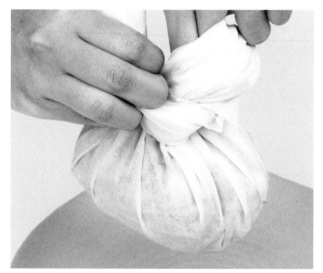

2 Take a 18-in (46-cm) square muslin cloth and put all the ingredients in the center of the cloth. Gather together the cloth and tie a knot around it.

3 Add this bouquet garni to the stock for mutton curries. Remove and discard the spices once the stock is prepared.

For this chutney, we use dried round purple or black plums, which are a different variety from the plums that are dried to make prunes. Due to its high sugar content, the chutney can be kept in the refrigerator for 2–3 months.

ALLOO BUKHARA CHATNEY

PLUM CHUTNEY   PAKISTAN

makes 2½ lb (1 kg)

3¾ cups sugar
1¼ lb (500 g) dried plums, soaked for 30 minutes and drained
small pinch of salt

small pinch of red chili powder
¼ tsp black peppercorns, crushed
good pinch of white cumin seeds
¼ oz (5 g) four seeds (p.28)

1 Put the sugar and 1¼ cups water in a large saucepan and bring to a boil, stirring to dissolve the sugar. Add the dried plums and cook for 20 minutes over medium heat.

2 Stir in the salt, red chili powder, crushed pepper, and cumin seeds. Mix in the four seeds. Allow to cool before serving or storage.

This *achar* (pickle) can be stored in a cool cupboard for 2–3 months or in the refrigerator for up to 6 months.

LASSAN ACHAR

PICKLED GARLIC   PAKISTAN

makes 2½ lb (1 kg)

½ cup white vinegar
3 tbsp salt
1 tbsp red chili powder
4 tsp ground turmeric

½ tsp black onion seeds
2 tbsp fennel seeds
1 tbsp fenugreek seeds
1¼ lb (500 g) garlic cloves, peeled
2 cups mustard oil

1 Combine the vinegar with the salt and all the spices in a large glass or ceramic jar. Add the garlic cloves. Leave in a cool place to marinate for 15 days.

2 Add the mustard oil and leave to marinate for a further 5–10 days or until the garlic cloves are slightly soft and have lost their pungent smell.

This is a fine example of one of the very hot chutneys and pickles that people consumed in the region of Rajasthan. These chutneys and pickles are often made from dried and preserved vegetables or fruit—here, *kachri*, a sour, tomatolike fruit, is used, adding texture as well as acidity and sharpness—and the heavy-handed spicing means that the chutney keeps for longer. In the old days, travelers would take these chutneys on their journeys and make a really tasty but simple meal of chutney and bread. This delicious chutney can be stored in the cupboard for a week, as long as it's covered by oil on top. It will keep for up to 2 weeks in the refrigerator. If you are unable to find *kachri*, you can increase the garlic by the same amount (9 oz/250 g). The result will be a much hotter chutney. Balance the flavor with 1 tbsp ketchup if it's too hot for your liking.

LAHSUN KI CHUTNEY

GARLIC CHUTNEY

NORTH INDIA—RAJASTHAN

makes about 1 lb (450 g)
hot, spicy, and sharp

1 cup vegetable or corn oil
1 tsp cumin seeds
5 oz (125 g) garlic, roughly chopped
2½ oz (75 g) dried red chilies, soaked in 1 cup water, drained, and made into a paste
⅓ cup malt vinegar
2 tbsp salt
1 tbsp red chili powder
9 oz (250 g) *kachri* (see above), coarsely pounded
3 tbsp sugar, or to taste
1 tbsp chopped cilantro leaves (optional)

1 Heat the oil in a saucepan, add the cumin seeds, and, when they crackle, add the garlic. Fry until it begins to turn golden.

2 Add the chili paste, vinegar, salt, and chili powder. Cook, stirring constantly, for 5–6 minutes. Add the *kachri*, if using, and cook the chutney for a further 12–15 minutes or until the fat separates out and comes to the top.

3 Check the seasoning and add the sugar, if required. Remove from the heat and allow to cool. This chutney can be eaten cold or hot. If you decide to heat it up before serving, add the fresh cilantro to liven it up.

The sharp and tangy taste of crushed mustard seeds blends perfectly with the creaminess of the thick yogurt. This combination acts as a wonderful appetizer that tantalizes the taste buds. It is also a perfect accompaniment to rich dishes, such as biryani and pilau.

MUSTARD RAITA

PAKISTAN

serves 4-5

1 tsp mustard seeds
9 oz (250 g) yogurt
salt
1 tsp black salt
1 tsp black peppercorns, coarsely crushed
1 tsp chopped cilantro leaves, plus extra for garnishing
pinch of red chili powder, for garnishing

1 Soak the mustard seeds in lukewarm water for an hour.

2 Meanwhile, whisk the yogurt in a bowl until thick and smooth.

3 Drain the water from the mustard seeds and grind them to a coarse paste with a mortar and pestle. Alternatively, you could use a food processor.

4 Add the mustard seed paste, both the salts, peppercorns, and cilantro to the yogurt and mix well. Garnish with red chili powder and the remaining cilantro.

DHANIA CHATNEY

CILANTRO CHUTNEY   PAKISTAN

Makes 12 oz (350 g)

5 oz (140 g) cilantro leaves
2 tbsp chopped green chilies
1 tsp red chili powder
salt

1 In a food processor or blender, purée the cilantro leaves with the green chilies to make a fine paste. Add a little water, if necessary.

2 Stir in the chili powder and salt to taste, and serve immediately.

NOTE Serve this chutney as soon as it is made to preserve its fresh green color.

SAIB CHATNEY

APPLE CHUTNEY   PAKISTAN

makes 1½ lb (600 g)

1¼ lb (500 g) green apples
lemon juice
1½ cups sugar
¼ tsp salt

small pinch of red chili powder
¼ tsp black peppercorns, crushed
1¼ tsp four seeds (p.28)

1 Peel and core the apples and cut into slices. Dip into a bowl of water mixed with lemon juice to prevent discoloration.

2 Put the sugar and ⅔ cup water in a large saucepan and bring to a boil, stirring to dissolve the sugar. Add the drained apple slices and cook over medium heat for 15 minutes or until the apples have softened.

3 Stir in the salt, red chili powder, crushed pepper, and four seeds. Allow to cool before serving.

NOTE This can be kept in the refrigerator in an airtight container for up to 2 months.

Use very unripe, green mangoes for this pickle. In a cooler climate, the marinating time may need to be extended—it can easily be doubled. All homemade pickles improve with age. Keep this in a cool place or the refrigerator.

AAM KA ACAR

MANGO PICKLE **PAKISTAN**

makes 2¼ lb (1 kg)

1¼ lb (500 g) small unripe
  mangoes
½ cup white vinegar
3 tbsp salt

1 tbsp red chili powder
4 tsp ground turmeric
½ tsp black onion seeds
2 tbsp fennel seeds
1 tbsp fenugreek seeds
2 cups mustard oil

1 Cut the unpeeled mangoes lengthwise into quarters, leaving the pits in.

2 Combine the vinegar, salt, and all the spices in a large glass or ceramic jar. Add the mangoes and stir. Leave to marinate in a cool place for 10–15 days or until the mangoes are slightly softened.

3 Add the mustard oil. Leave to marinate for a further 5–10 days before using.

Popular during the winter months, when fresh herbs and other vegetables are scarce, cumin raita has an aromatic, mildly spicy flavor. It's great with meat, fish, and seafood curries and goes well with all rice dishes, too.

ZEERA RAITA

CUMIN RAITA   **PAKISTAN**

serves 4-5

8 oz (225 g) plain Greek-style
   yogurt
½ tsp salt
½ tsp white cumin seeds

Whisk the yogurt in a bowl to be sure it is well combined and thick, then add the salt and cumin seeds, mixing well. Chill for at least 30 minutes before serving.

Mint has a wonderful aromatic fragrance and flavor, and it gives yogurt a beautiful green color, which is why this is the most popular of all the raitas. It enhances the flavor of the food it accompanies and also acts as a palate cleanser between each bite.

PODINA RAITA

MINT RAITA   **PAKISTAN**

serves 4-5

8 oz (225 g) plain Greek-style
   yogurt
salt to taste

¼ cup finely chopped
   mint leaves
1 tsp finely chopped
   green chili

Whisk the yogurt in a bowl to be sure it is well combined and thick, then add the salt, chopped mint, and green chili, mixing well. Chill for at least 30 minutes before serving.

With its sharp onion flavor, this raita is a good partner for curries made from vegetables, lentils, and beans. It also goes well with rice dishes.

PIYAZ RAITA

ONION RAITA — PAKISTAN

serves 4-5

8 oz (225 g) plain Greek-style
    yogurt
¼ cup finely chopped onion,
    squeezed dry
½ tsp crushed dried chilies
salt

Whisk the yogurt in a bowl to be sure it is well combined and thick, then add the onion, crushed chilies, and salt to taste, mixing well. Chill for at least 30 minutes before serving.

Cucumber raita is very popular during the summer months, as it is known for its cooling properties. Serve it with vegetable and bean curries. It is also delicious eaten on its own with a fresh salad.

KHEERA RAITA

CUCUMBER RAITA — PAKISTAN

serves 4-5

8 oz (225 g) plain Greek-style
    yogurt
4 tbsp grated cucumber,
    squeezed dry
½ tsp red chili powder
salt

Whisk the yogurt in a bowl to be sure it is well combined and thick, then add the cucumber, chili powder, and salt to taste, mixing well. Chill for at least 30 minutes before serving.

GLOSSARY

ASIAN CELERY
Also known as wild celery, this has a very strong, bitter flavor. Similar in appearance to flat-leaf parsley, it is often used as a flavoring in stir-fries and soups.

BAI YOR LEAF
Otherwise known as Indian mulberry leaf, this is a tobaccolike plant with a bitter, earthy flavor. In Thailand and the Philippines, young *bai yor* leaves may be shredded and added to curries. It is not readily available in the West.

BETEL LEAF
These are used in Thailand, predominantly as an edible wrapping for certain hors d'oeuvres. They can be replaced with spinach leaves.

BIRYANI
The original Persian spelling is *biriani*, meaning "fried," and refers to a spicy dish of meat and basmati rice flavored with saffron. The Moghul version was often elaborately garnished with gold leaf.

CHA-OM
Not widely available in the West, this green herb is in fact the leaves of the Thai acacia tree. It has a bitter, nutty flavor and is commonly used in Laos and Thailand in soups, curries, omelets, and stir-fries.

CHOY SUM OR CHOI SUM
Also known as Chinese flowering cabbage, this is a very popular vegetable in Cantonese cuisine, as well as being widely used throughout Asia and the West. It is sold as bunches of leaves and can be used raw in salads or lightly boiled or steamed to add to meat dishes.

DAL
This can refer to either split lentils (or other legumes) as an ingredient, or, more generically, to a dish containing beans, peas, or lentils.

HALWA OR HALVA
Derived from the Arabic word for sweet (*hulw*) in India, *halwa* refers to a semolina and sugar-based confectionery. The ingredients and flavorings vary widely, with the simplest recipe involving semolina being fried in ghee with syrup and raisins. In Pakistan, meanwhile, *halva* can be similar in texture and appearance to Turkish delight.

JACKFRUIT
A large fruit native to Southern India but grown all over India and Sri Lanka. When unripe, it is treated more as a vegetable and added to savory dishes. As it ripens, it becomes much sweeter and is mainly used in desserts.

KADHAI OR KARAHI
Kadhai, or karahi, refers to an Indian wok, and also the dish it produces, namely a stir-fry. This rapid method of cooking is popular with youngsters and amateur chefs who do not want to spend hours in the kitchen.

KORMA
A cooking term that, in India and Pakistan, originally referred to a slow-cooked dish with a sauce. Nuts, yogurt, and butter are the ingredients most commonly used to enrich an Indian korma.

MASALA OR MASSALLA
Meaning "spice mixture," masala can refer to any combination of spices, ground or whole, hot or mild, as a powder or paste. These mixes form the basis for most Indian dishes and vary widely from region to region. Garam masala (p.167) is the best-known example, though again, the blend will differ according to regional preferences. In terms of preparations, powders are generally preferred in North India, while pastes are favored in the south.

MIRIN
Similar in appearance to rice wine, *mirin* is a liquid sweetener used in Japanese cuisine. It is only used in very small quantities, often in the place of sugar and soy sauce. It has a low alcohol content, and in the

17th and 18th centuries, it was even drunk as an alternative to sake.

PANDANUS LEAF
An important ingredient throughout Southeast Asia, predominantly as a flavoring in Thai, Malaysian, and Indonesian cooking. They are added directly to rice dishes and desserts, allowing their delicate fragrance to infuse the food. The leaves should be bought fresh where possible, though they can be found frozen or dried.

POPADUM OR PAPADUM
These are thin, round wafers made from dough and fried in oil until crisp. Chickpea flour and lentil flour are both commonly used, and various spices may also be added. In North India, they tend to be spicier, whereas in the south, a milder recipe is preferred to balance the hotter local cuisine.

RAITA
This is a cooling, yogurt-based condiment that is popular as an accompaniment to fiery curries. The yogurt is seasoned with herbs and spices, including mustard, cumin, mint, and cilantro. In addition, various chopped vegetables may be added; cucumber is popular in western versions, though eggplant, potato, and spinach are just as popular in authentic Indian *raita*.

RICE VINEGAR
Most Asian vinegars are brewed from rice; they have a lower acid content than malt vinegars and are relatively mild. Japanese brown rice vinegar is the best quality but is not easy to find.

SHOYU
An essential ingredient in Japanese cuisine, *shoyu* is a soy sauce that strongly differs in flavor from its Chinese counterpart. This is due to the presence of wheat, which gives the Japanese sauce a sweeter, more alcoholic taste.

SIAMESE WATERCRESS
More commonly known in the West as water spinach and in Thailand as *pak bung*, this leafy vegetable has excellent nutritional qualities. Full of protein and minerals, it is an inexpensive addition for curries and stir-fries.

SNAKE BEANS
Also known as yard-long beans, these are excellent eaten raw when very fresh and firm. They can be used as a garnish or lightly cooked in stir-fries.

SUGAR CANE VINEGAR
Popular in the Philippines, this vinegar is mild in flavor, not dissimilar to rice vinegar. It is dark yellow or brown in color and, unusually, is not at all sweet.

TANDOOR
Essential to the way of life in North India and Pakistan, the *tandoor* is a clay oven used to bake breads and other dishes. It is the focal point of many homes, and some villages may even have a communal *tandoor* where gossip is as important as cooking. The fires are fueled by charcoal and are often kept lit all day.

TAWA OR TAVA
A flat, circular pan, often made from cast iron, used in Indian cooking to make *chapattis* and *parathas*.

INDEX

ACKNOWLEDGMENTS

DORLING KINDERSLEY WOULD LIKE TO THANK THE FOLLOWING:

Updated edition 2015

Tanvi Mishra for new photography; Deeba Rajpal for food and prop styling; Aditya Kapoor for his studio space; Nandita Talukder for her props; Roopam Baijal, Harnoor Channi-Tiwary, and Madhumita Mitra for recipe testing; Gazal Bawa and Vikas Sachdeva for design assistance; Tarika and Anuja Naorem for editorial assistance; Sreshtha Bhattacharya, Pallavi Paul, Neha Samuel, Suparna Sengupta, and Kriti Talwar for proofreading and Aparajita Barai and Namita for assistance.

2015 Edition: DK UK, Managing Editor Dawn Henderson, Managing Art Editor Christine Keilty, Senior Jacket Creative Nicola Powling, Pre-production Producer Dragana Puvacic, Senior Producer Jen Scothern, Art Director Peter Luff, Category Publisher Peggy Vance; DK India, Senior Art Editor Ira Sharma, Project Lead Editor Arani Sinha, Project Art Editor Anjan Dey, Managing Editor Alicia Ingty, Deputy Managing Editor Bushra Ahmed, Managing Art Editor Navidita Thapa, DTP Designers Rajdeep Singh, Manish Upreti, Pre-production Manager Sunil Sharma

First edition 2006

Jeni Wright and Norma Macmillan for their tireless hard work and professionalism; Food stylists: Bridget Sargeson and Alice Hart; Prop stylist: Victoria Allen; Index: Hilary Bird; DTP: Adam Walker and Emma Hansen-Knarhoi; On behalf of David Thompson: Tanongsak Yordwai, who prepared and styled David's food for photography.

2006 Edition: Commissioning Editor Jeni Wright, Art Director Peter Luff, Project Manager and Editor Norma Macmillan, Creative Publisher Mary-Clare Jerram, Senior Art Editor Susan Dowing, Operations Publishing Manager Gillian Roberts, Senior Editor Dawn Henderson, Publisher Corrine Roberts, Project Art Editor Caroline de Souza, Photographic Art Director Simon Daley, DTP Designers Adam Walker, Traci Salter, Designer Sue Storey, Production Controller Stuart Masheter, Editorial Assistant Zoe Moore, Photographer Hugh Johnson

CONTRIBUTORS

Vivek Singh

Vivek is a renowned chef, author, and restauranteur. He is the CEO and Executive Chef of five modern Indian restaurants (four in London, one in Oxford), including his flagship restaurant, The Cinnamon Club, located in the grand former Westminster Library. Outside of the kitchen, he has authored several acclaimed cookbooks, including *Spice at Home* and *Indian Festival Feasts*, and is a regular on BBC's *Saturday Kitchen* and *Celebrity Masterchef*, as well as at live cooking events across the UK. Following his childhood in West Bengal, Vivek was classically trained as a chef in Delhi and worked for the prestigious Oberoi hotel group in India before he moved to London in 2001.

His innovative approach to combining flavors, ingredients, and techniques from East and West has placed him at the vanguard of a new style of Indian fine dining and made him one of the most inspiring chefs of his generation.

G. Sultan Mohideenh

Winner of several awards, which include the Chef De Cuisine Award in 1995, the Chef of the Year Award in 1998, and the Culinary Czar of Indian Cuisine Award in 2006 and 2014, Sultan is no stranger to accolades. After completing his postgraduation from the Oberoi School of Hotel Management, New Delhi, he went on to work in premier five-star hotels, establishing himself as an institution in Indian cuisine. He has the distinction of having catered for 30 world leaders, including the Clintons and Tony Blair. His research on the gastronomical heritage of the Dravidian Kingdoms of Pandiya, Chera, and Tippu Sultan's Kingdom earned him the Dr. Ambedkar Puraskar award from the Karnataka government. He also has a book to his name, *Samiyal Sultan*, which is a collection of his weekly columns in the Tamil magazine, *Ananda Vikatan*. He has featured in the *New York Times* and in *The International Who's Who of Chefs 2004–2005*, published by IWWC.

Das Sreedharan

Das is the founding chef of Rasa restaurants in London. Since starting up in 1994, he has created a new awareness of regional Indian cuisine. With a humble upbringing, Das learned traditional cooking skills and vegetable gardening from his mother. Now, through his restaurants, he passionately champions the simple, subtle flavors of Keralan food, offering his customers a fresh alternative to typical curry-house dishes. Das has published three cookbooks about his native cuisine and organizes annual festivals promoting Indian food and culture. He conducts weekly classes in London and has recently launched a cooking school in India, teaching traditional techniques. Through the school, he aims to encourage healthy home cooking and ethical living. Das lives in London, taking regular trips to Kerala to seek new flavors and seasonings for his customers' delight.

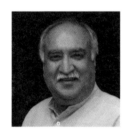

Mahmood Akbar

From an early age, Mahmood was exposed to the pleasures of food and cooking by both his father, a great food lover, and his mother, an excellent cook. He obtained his degree in hotel management in the US, then joined Hilton International, where he spent five years as a food and beverage manager, including time in Hong Kong and East Asia. In 1982, Mahmood decided to start up his own restaurants, including the now-famous Salt 'n Pepper Village restaurants in Lahore and Karachi. In his business, he is assisted by his wife and, recently, by his daughter, who also graduated in the US with a hotel management degree. Mahmood's passion for food is undiminished. The lesson he learned as a child from his father about using only the freshest ingredients has become his guiding principle in running his own restaurants: all food is purchased fresh every morning and consumed the same day.

DK UK
Senior Editor Dawn Titmus
Senior Art Editor Glenda Fisher
Editorial Assistant Millie Andrew
US Editor Kayla Dugger
Jacket Designers Amy Cox, Saffron Stocker
Jackets Coordinator Lucy Philpott
Pre-production Producer David Almond
Senior Producer Stephanie McConnell
Managing Editor Ruth O'Rourke
Managing Art Editor Christine Keilty
Art Director Maxine Pedliham
Publishing Director Mary-Clare Jerram

DK INDIA
Senior Editor Janashree Singha
Project Editor Dipika Dasgupta
Editors Rishi Bryan, Avanika
Managing Editor Soma B. Chowdhury
Senior DTP Designers Pushpak Tyagi, Tarun Sharma
DTP Designers Satish Gaur, Anurag Trivedi
Pre-production Manager Sunil Sharma

This American Edition, 2020
First American Edition, 2006
Published in the United States by DK Publishing
1450 Broadway, Suite 801, New York, NY 10018
20 21 22 23 10 9 8 7 6 5 4 3 2 1
001-318704-Oct/2020

A catalog record for this book
is available from the Library of Congress.
ISBN 978-1-4654-9941-7

Printed and bound in China

For the curious
www.dk.com